OTTO PÄCHT

BOOK ILLUMINATION
IN THE MIDDLE AGES

OTTO PÄCHT

BOOK ILLUMINATION IN THE MIDDLE AGES

AN INTRODUCTION

with a Preface
by J. J. G. Alexander

HARVEY MILLER PUBLISHERS
OXFORD UNIVERSITY PRESS

HARVEY MILLER PUBLISHERS
20 Marryat Road · London · SW 19 5 BD · England

Published in conjunction with
OXFORD UNIVERSITY PRESS
Walton Street · Oxford

London · Glasgow · New York · Toronto · Melbourne · Auckland
Kuala Lumpur · Singapore · Hong Kong · Tokyo · Delhi · Bombay · Calcutta · Madras · Karachi
Nairobi · Dar es Salaam · Cape Town · and associates in Beirut · Ibadan · Mexico City · Nicosia

Published in the United States by
OXFORD UNIVERSITY PRESS · New York

Originally published in German as *Buchmalerei des Mittelalters*
Eine Einführung, edited by Dagmar Thoss and Ulrike Jenni
by Prestel-Verlag Munich, 1984
First English translation published by Harvey Miller, London, 1986

Translated from the German by Kay Davenport

British Library Cataloguing in Publication Data
Pächt, Otto
    Book illumination in the Middle Ages :
    an introduction.
    1. Illumination of books and manuscripts,
    Medieval   2. Illumination of books
    and manuscripts, Renaissance
    I. Title   II. Buchmalerei des Mittelalters.
    English
    745.6'7   ND2920

    ISBN 0-19-921060-8

© 1984 Prestel-Verlag Munich
© 1986 English Translation – Harvey Miller
Colour origination: Ernst Wartelsteiner, Garching near Munich
Monochrome origination: Brend'Amour, Simhart & Co., Munich
Set, printed and bound by Passavia Druckerei GmbH, Passau
Manufactured in West Germany

Contents

Acknowledgements

The Publishers wish to express their gratitude to all who have helped with the publication of this book: to those who have made photographs available for reproduction and to those who have been kind enough to give valuable advice in the course of production. In particular thanks are due to Jonathan Alexander, Janet Backhouse, Michael Evans, Elisabeth Klemm, Tilly de la Mare, Florentine Mütherich, Jörg Oberhaidacher and Gertraut Schikola.

The Publishers also wish to thank Professor Otto Pächt for his most helpful supervision of the English translation; and they are deeply grateful to his son Michael Pächt for producing the volume with such devoted care and elegance.

Preface

OTTO PÄCHT has always stressed, as he does at the beginning of this book, that manuscript illumination is an autonomous art form with its own separate tradition. It is not to be thought of as a minor branch of the history of painting and of interest only in so far as it reflects the supposedly more major art. Pächt argues in his introduction that the reason illumination has been taken less seriously than other forms of painting is because of the failure to develop a proper critical theory in relation to it. Nevertheless book illumination is now more generally accepted as an object of study in its own right, and this is largely the result of the work of scholars of Pächt's generation, and due not least to his own publications and teaching.

His scholarly work as manifested in books, articles and lectures produced over more than sixty years has been concerned with the most diverse periods and schools, as well as with theoretical matters such as the identification of the characteristics of national styles, for example in Flemish and French art in the fifteenth century, or the development of a particular genre of art, for example landscape art, or the problems associated with the creation of religious narrative art in the Middle Ages. These wide interests are by no means confined to manuscript illumination, for his earliest work was on the Flemish painters of the fifteenth century, and they give the present book its breadth of scope and its maturity of outlook. Though the special nature of book illumination is always in the foreground in this book, that certainly does not mean that illumination is seen in isolation. On the contrary, its development is always placed in the wider context of other contemporary art forms and cultural developments.

Pächt is a foremost member of the Viennese school of art history which already from the time of Wickhoff and Riegl, a hundred years ago, interested itself in book illumination. One crucial feature of Riegl's work was his attention to forms of art seen then as minor or decorative, for example in his books *Stilfragen* of 1893 and *Spätrömische Kunstindustrie* of 1901. Another was the attention to periods of art history which at that time were perceived as in decline from the 'great' periods, particularly the Late Antique and the Baroque. Pächt equally in this present book is not concerned to set up one school or period against another, still less to impose value judgements. He stresses the importance of the initials, the framing devices and the page lay-out as equally vital and creative parts of the illuminators' work with the figural miniatures.

There are perhaps two fundamental preoccupations which lie behind this account as they do behind Riegl's work. The way in which human beings' involvement with the three-dimensional world in which they move is represented (re-presented) in art is the first concern. Particular artistic styles deal with the problems of representation in particular ways which it is the art historians' task to analyse. In pictorial art, for example, the relationship established between the surface of the picture, which is two-dimensional and bounded, and the pictorial representation of objects within the picture is crucial. Secondly the requirements of a particular medium produce particular problems for the artist. The solutions to these formal problems interrelate with the purpose of the work of art. That purpose can be rather narrowly defined in terms of its physical context or setting which dictates how it is seen, but may also embrace wider considerations of historical or cultural change. From this it follows, to give just one example treated by Pächt, that the painting and decoration in the roll form of book in the Ancient World is different from that in the codex form of book which as a matter of history succeeded it at the beginning of the post-classical period. It is different first because the forms of classical art are different, for example in the representation of space or in the categorical differentiation of ornament and narrative figural art which in later medieval art can physically intermingle. But it is also different, Pächt argues, because the action of unfurling the roll makes the perception of the pictures it contains different from that of the perception of the static bounded pages of the codex. The picture or the decoration on the page of the codex is thereby affected formally.

From this it will be clear that Pächt's *Book Illumination,* wide-ranging though it is, does not aim to be a descriptive account of various schools, and it does not follow a chronological order. It offers instead a stylistic analysis and ways of seeing in context various forms of book illumination. It starts logically, for instance, by discussing the initial where script, decoration and picture come together most closely. These close relationships provided the illuminator with a series of opportunities but also a series of problems which are solved in various ways at various times. Particular solutions as well as artistic developments outside the domain of illumination in turn produce new problems so that at certain times and in certain areas the initial is a major vehicle for artistic creativity, at others less so. In Italy in the 12th-century Giant Bibles, for example, the hegemony of monumental art meant that narrative images were more likely to remain independent rather than be incorporated in the initials.

Pächt's aim is to open our eyes to be fully attentive and responsive to the work of art. So the illustrations of the book are not an optional extra to an argument which could stand without them. They are chosen with all the perceptiveness and the insight of an extraordinarily richly filled visual memory. Another inheritance of the Vienna School is the emphasis on the closest possible acquaintance with works of art examined in detail and at first hand. Pächt's familiarity with medieval works of art of all kinds is immense and probably unequalled. Illuminated manuscripts especially are works of art which are both widely scattered and difficult of access, so the book and its illustrations are also the product of an unique experience of searching out and scrutinizing them in libraries and collections all over the world.

Thus to have Pächt as it were looking over one's shoulder at an illuminated manuscript in this way, is to be able to share that experience and to have one's eyes opened to a richer and clearer seeing. The reader should look, for example, at the two church interiors of the early fifteenth century reproduced in figures 208-9 and then look at them again in reading Pächt's comments.

Though acknowledging the necessity of words in the analysis of the work of art, Pächt tends to distrust rhetorical overelaborations as a distraction. In this book the words, so carefully chosen, contain original and characteristic insights brilliantly and concisely expressed. But analysis and commentary are only a means to an end. We must let the work of art speak to us, not lecture at it. The aim, to use a favourite expression of Pächt's, is not to speak oneself in front of the work of art, but to listen with the eyes.

J. J. G. Alexander

Introduction

Many decades ago, when I was a student, the study of illuminated manuscripts – miniature painting – was generally considered to be a sign of modesty inasmuch as one was content to allow one's academic ambition to be confined to a by-water of art-historical scholarship. If one became more familiar with the subject, one could expect to be called a 'specialist', by which was meant an eccentric rather than an expert, or at best, a master in a minor art. An exception was made for those who dealt with Carolingian or Ottonian illumination, because it was the only kind of painting to have survived from these great periods of medieval culture.

Today, the situation is not quite so constricted. Illuminated manuscripts, and those who study them, are more respected. Miniature painting is no longer regarded as a poor surrogate of major works of art which have been lost. However, even today less value is attached to the art of illuminators than that to that of their colleagues who worked on a large scale. In theory, the special character of illumination as an art-form is now recognized, yet the study of it has been so long eclipsed by the more traditional branches of art history that it has failed to develop a proper critical apparatus. We still tend to look at illuminated manuscripts with eyes too much conditioned by wall and panel painting to interpret them correctly. This is most clearly revealed in the type of illumination generally reproduced in books on history of art. A volume which appeared in 1929 as part of a lavishly illustrated manual of art history[1] devotes 125 plates to early medieval illumination, but includes no more than three initials – so that one of the most original manifestations of medieval fantasy is virtually unrepresented – and the choice of plates is limited solely to miniatures. Furthermore, in book illustration, the differences between miniature painting and monumental art – which are not only a matter of format – become blurred, especially when, as often happens, miniatures and details are enlarged to the point where the pictorial surface seems to resemble painting techniques found elsewhere. So it is probably inevitable that manuscript illumination continues to be looked upon as a stunted form of monumental art, even by those who fully understand that the name of 'miniature' painting originates not from 'diminuere' (to reduce) but from 'minium', a frequently-used red pigment.

The unfortunate fact that Greek monumental painting has been almost entirely lost to us has enabled classical archaeologists, when discussing and analyzing the corresponding 'miniature' art – vase painting – to avoid the trap of erroneously applying criteria imported from outside sources. They have remained aware of the differences between the decoration of a vase and the painting of a wall, and know that the vase painter, like anyone who worked with a minimum of ornamental vocabulary, was always mindful of the structural restriction in the task at hand, that of decorating a vessel. Manuscript illumination had to deal with entirely similar problems, and its starting point is not simply the individual composition of a book in quires but also the object as a whole, in this case the book as an organism with its own special configuration.

From its beginnings, in contrast to Greek vase painting, the book contained a dual interaction between functional structure and external form, its ornamentation. Besides the formal and physical properties of the book, there was an integral spiritual aspect, namely that contained in the script – those conventional but symbolic signs which were living testimony to the intellectual content acting through them – the text. The relationship between physical and non-physical, or form and content, is not something purely rational, like the correlation of text and illustration. It is irrational and magical. In an age when the most important book, the Book of Books, was the Holy Scripture, the believer, even if illiterate, instinctively felt this deeper meaning in the relationship between the book and its outward form, its artistic embellishment.

It is this aspect of the medieval book that helps to explain the aesthetic quality of its decoration and illumination. In the Christian Middle Ages, the book was not merely an object, a thing to be used: it had its own special meaning as witness to the promise of salvation, and in this respect was scarcely less potent a symbol than the Cross. The book in itself had a luminous aura, as can be seen in the etymology of the word 'bible', from 'biblion', which originally meant book in the form of a papyrus roll, but which the Middle Ages appropriated for one book, Holy Scripture. In most profound contrast to classical culture, Christianity was a religion whose focus was the Book. One need only think of those innumerable Crucifixions in which the beloved John is represented, standing at the foot of the Cross at the hour of Sacrifice, in deepest grief, and in his hand, the Book (fig. 1).[2] It would be quite impossible to imagine a classical image of Apollo in which the god was shown holding a papyrus roll of Homer's Hymn to Apollo. Christianity, however, drew no distinction between the book as an instrument of communication and the message it conveyed. The book was the source of faith made palpable: it not only contained the Gospel, it *was* the Gospel.

This sanctity of the book as Gospel was indissolubly linked to its special function in authenticating the history of Christianity. The Gospels a missionary brought with him and from which he preached, the Gospels of any missionary renowned for converting the heathen barbarians – St. Patrick for the Irish, for example, or St. Augustine

I
Crucifixion.
Andreas-Altar Missal,
St. Florian, c. 1320

of Canterbury for the Anglo-Saxons, or St. Boniface for the Germans
– the book these saints possessed (or were reputed to have possessed),
was inevitably venerated as a relic of these saints and became in effect
a national shrine.

One such book which has remained in England is known as the
Gospels of St. Augustine of Canterbury (fig. 36);[3] we know that until
the late Middle Ages it was kept not in the Library at Canterbury but
actually lay on the altar; it belonged, in other words, like a reliquary
or the Cross, to Church ceremonial. In a similar manner, other books
attached to missionary saints were fundamentally regarded as relics
and preserved in costly metal shrines. These are the oldest reliquaries
from the North. The Gospels known as the Book of Durrow (pl. II,
fig. 83) which, according to a colophon, belonged to St. Columba,
missionary of the Picts,[4] is said to have been enshrined in this way.[5]

2
'Soiscél Molaise' Reliquary.
Insular, 9th century

One of the oldest Irish examples of such a reliquary is the shrine of 'Soiscél Molaise' (fig. 2), which contains the Gospels of St. Molaise, an Irish missionary of the sixth century.[6]

In the regions of northern Europe which were untouched by classical culture, without any literary tradition, and only Christianized in the early Middle Ages – regions of nomadic and illiterate peoples – the book from the beginning bore the charged atmosphere of a higher world; consequently, the illuminated book offered far greater stimulus to artistic activity and achievement in the North than it did in Mediterranean regions, where it had never exercised so prominent a role.

What we are considering here is a book that poses particular artistic problems and offers special formal solutions. It must be remembered, however, that the transition to a wholly distinctive genre, the codex, already found in late Antiquity, was the prerequisite of all subsequent and unique artistic developments associated with that form – the transition from roll to codex, into what we today understand by 'book': single pages of the same format of text sequentially arranged rather than continuously written, in other words the change from a scroll which is unrolled to a book which is opened and leafed through.

3
St. Luke.
Gospels.
Byzantine, mid 10th century

4
Attic stele.
5th century B.C.

A visual record of this change from roll to codex can be found in a tenth-century Byzantine miniature (based on a sixth-century model), which depicts the Evangelist Luke writing in a *codex* on his lap but obviously transcribing from a *roll* which is unfurled across his lectern (fig. 3).[7] The same manuscript shows in its picture of the Evangelist John (fig. 16) a codex open on the lectern, while on the floor near by several rolls are visible in a container.[8] How rolls were handled is widely attested. On an Attic stele of the fifth century B.C. (fig. 4), for example, we can see how the roll was held with one hand while the other hand pulled, and at the same time un-rolled and re-rolled the text being read.

In the antique world the normal writing material was papyrus: the roll was made of papyrus. But the latter is a relatively impermanent substance, not suitable for any lasting purposes; and papyri, as is well known, could be obtained only from Egypt because of its dry climate. When, in the third century B.C., transcriptions of the Hebrew Old

Testament were given to Greek-speaking Jews living in Alexandria
for the purpose of translating into Greek, the original Hebrew text,
written on animal membrane, appears in the Greek translation (the
Septuagint) in papyrus rolls. When working methods were developed
which substantially refined the animal membrane that had already
been in use as writing material, the first serious rival to papyrus was
parchment. But as long as rolls were the chief requirement, parchment
was at a disadvantage: it was more difficult to unroll than the more
flexible, lighter papyrus. A further innovation was needed to give
victory to parchment: the introduction of the codex, the paged book.

The prototype of the codex was the two-fold wooden panel,
familiar to us as the diptych. Its insides were coated with wax upon
which a stylus was used to incise short notes or memoranda in law
courts or on other occasions. In the so-called Probianus Diptych, for
example (fig. 5), the small figures on either side of the enthroned
saint write on such two-fold panels; in contrast, the other figures
represented in the lower compartments hold rolls.

From the first century, A.D. onwards, there is evidence in Rome
of the existence of books with pages (called 'membranae'), which
were probably of small format ('libelli'). It has recently been further
established that the Christian community actively favoured codices
in paper at an early date, certainly by the second century; in other
words, there was a change towards the codex but to one made
with cheap writing material. Christian literature appeared in cheap
'publications', because these were the unostentatious books used by
an underground sect whose members were also dedicated to unworld-
liness. Classical pagan literature continued to be issued in the form of
rolls as it always had been. Indeed, it appears that up to the time
when Christianity was officially recognized, Christians deliberately
endorsed the codex in protest against pagan usage of the roll, not only
classical but also Jewish, as in the Torah Roll.[9] When Christianity

4a
Dead Sea Scroll – Isaiah.
First century B.C.

5
Probianus Diptych.
Rome, c. 400

was elevated to a state religion under Constantine in the fourth century, the codex format became the norm for all literature. In the course of that century, the decisive process of transferring classical and Christian literature from papyrus roll to parchment book was broadly completed – a process of enormous importance for the survival of our classical heritage and the development of European consciousness. It began out of a desire to conserve: the life of a papyrus roll was short. If something written on papyrus lasted two hundred years, it was regarded as a miracle. Had there been no transition to parchment, there would not have been even the material conditions necessary for the survival of classical literature. The period which spanned that past and the future would have become intensely narrow and restrictive, since only those things which stood above changes in public taste or the vagaries of public interest, and only those things held to be eternal, would have been passed down from generation to generation. In practice, in post-classical times, this would only have been the Holy Scriptures, the Bible. Victory of the codex over the roll signified the rescue of the classical past for posterity.

Naturally, the rescue effected by this process was highly selective. Only what in the fourth and fifth centuries seemed worth reading, only what was of actual interest at that time, made the journey from roll into codex and thus survived. In essence, the criteria were twofold: firstly, which classical authors and which of their texts should future generations read in the original; and secondly, which should at most be referred to by name or title? The width or narrowness of those tastes have determined our own intellectual horizons. Furthermore, it is well known that this was not the only process of selectivity which the classical tradition had to undergo. A number of external factors peculiar to the time placed the rescue of late-antique literature, and the work of any scribe, in jeopardy – the decline, or rather the collapse of Mediterranean civilization, its political impotence and the invasion of Islam. As a result, it fell to that first Renaissance of western Europe, in the Carolingian period, to rescue what remained to be rescued from the classical heritage by its prolific activity in the transcription of classical texts. It is obvious that, at this point, the reservoir from which knowledge of Christian literature could be drawn had severely diminished. The geographical centre of the Carolingian Renaissance was upon lands which belonged to ancient Gaul. Monastic scriptoria, which were responsible for the transcriptions of texts, could in the ordinary course of events only obtain texts available locally, that is, in the libraries of ancient Gaul, although there were isolated instances of borrowing from other countries. Added to the restriction of what was actually available to the new Carolingian Empire, there was a further force actively reducing the selection of texts to be copied,

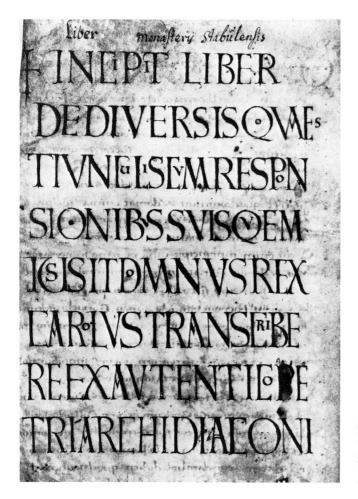

6
Incipit to
Liber de diversis quaestiunculis
by Peter the Archdeacon.
Aachen, late 8th century

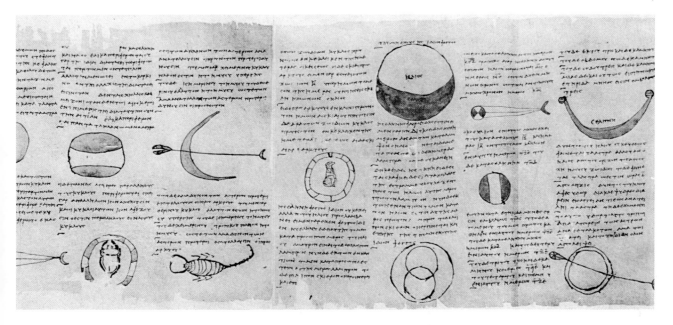

7
Commentary on Celestial Bodies.
Astrological papyrus roll, 165 B.C.

dictated by the interest and taste of the new monastic readership. It was indeed exceptional to find Carolingian textual transcriptions which combined the satisfaction of spiritual interests with the wider intellectual horizons which prevailed at the court of Charlemagne intent on enriching a secular library. A notable example of this profane contribution to the process of saving the intellectual baggage of Antiquity is the 'Liber de diversis quaestiunculis' of Peter the Archdeacon; the Incipit (fig. 6) explains, in the majuscule lettering thought at the time to be appropriately classical, that Charlemagne personally ordered the work to be transcribed, 'Here begins the book of Divers Trifling Questions with their Replies which Lord King Charles ordered to be transcribed ...'

In these remarks on the content of a manuscript we seem to have strayed from our proper theme, the form and transformation of the medieval book. Let me revert to it. To understand fully the genesis of medieval illumination, it is the first process of transcription from roll to codex, which took place in late Antiquity, that is of major importance. In copying a text, the content remained unaltered. This was indeed the purpose of the activity. Only errors in transcription created changes. But what about the kind of script, and where relevant, the physical characteristics of the decoration and illustration? Was it desirable or was it plausible to reproduce or copy them? Could these aspects even be transcribed without their being altered? One need only ask such questions to realise the practical and technical problems involved in this matter of transcription.

Papyrus rolls were written in many long, narrow columns consisting of short lines (fig. 7). In transferring a strip of continous script of considerable length to a sequence of relatively small separate pages, two to four of such columns at the most could be fitted on to one page (figs. 8, 9). It used to be thought that the juxtaposition of several columns of text on the page of a book was due to the arrangement of text found in the roll, which was appropriate to the roll; and that in the book it betrayed a lack of freedom, since it was rooted in a tradition developed in an organically different medium. As we are now aware of the special significance which Early Christians attached to the codex, another explanation seems more plausible: Early Christian codices, made of paper, were modest in size and most probably had, as a rule, only a single column of script with lines slightly wider than would be usual in the text columns of rolls. But luxury editions of the Bible, on parchment – for example, the famous Codex Sinaiticus (fig. 9), written in four columns, one of the few *de luxe* Bibles of late Antiquity to have survived almost intact – could be interpreted as the result of a deliberate attempt to classicize, with the aristocracy, the ruling class, in mind; in other words, it was an instance of the Christian book adapting itself to values still rooted in the pagan past.

8
Signs of the Zodiac. Treatise
on Chronology and Astronomy.
Salzburg, c. 818

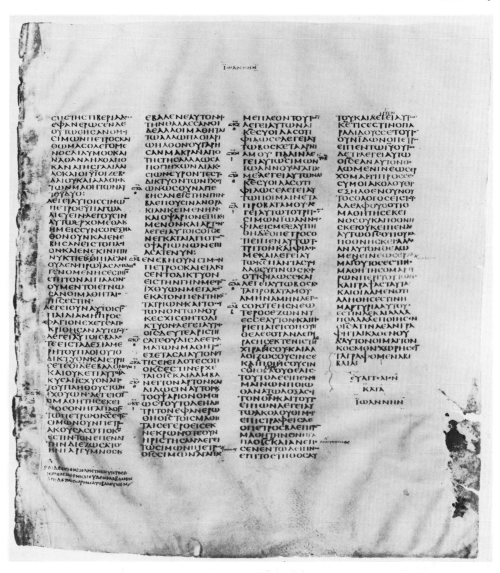

9
Explicit of St. John's Gospel.
Codex Sinaiticus, 4th century

The addition of further columns to the page in Carolingian times, for example in the Utrecht Psalter (fig. 10), or later, was doubtless motivated by a desire to give special decorum and a classical appearance to the manuscript. Thus the Utrecht Psalter, instead of using contemporary minuscule, is written in majuscules, classical capitals. By the early eleventh century, the Anglo-Saxon copy of it (pl. XVIII) had abandoned this affectation, and in its line-drawings substituted colour for monochrome, another modernization. In a second copy made in England in the twelfth century,[10] further modern justification was found for multi-columns: it was presented as a triple psalterium, that is, a concordance of the three Latin versions of the Psalter (fig. 11, the beginning of Psalm 11, which shows three versions of the same text: 'Salva me ...'; 'Salvum me fac ...').

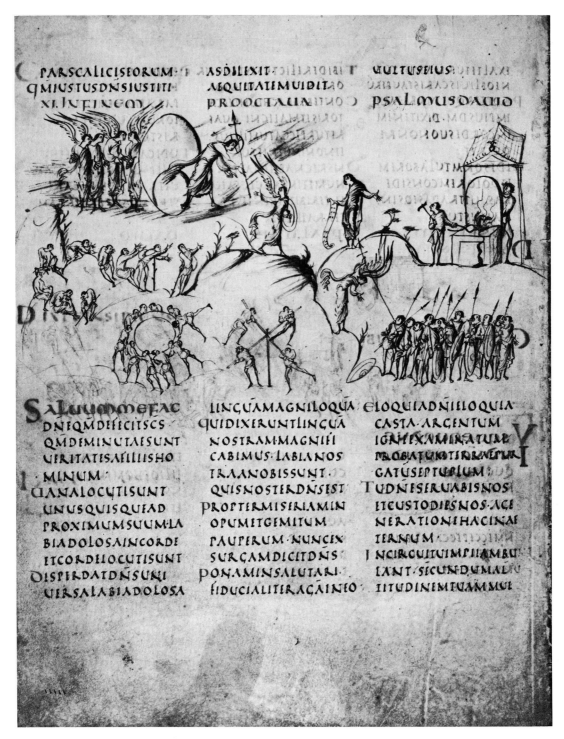

10
Illustration to Psalm 11.
Utrecht Psalter.
Reims, c. 830

11
Illustration to Psalm 11.
Eadwine Psalter.
Canterbury, c. 1150

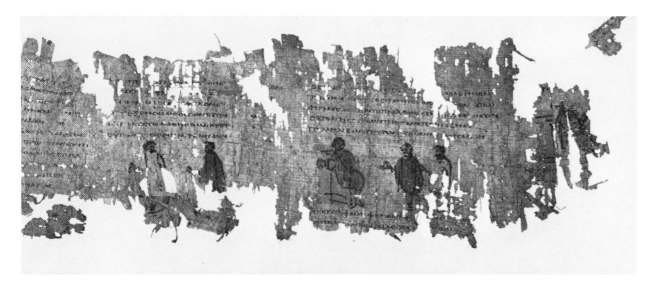

The rescue of the literary legacy of Antiquity was largely due to the parchment codex; but what about the actual appearance of that legacy, its embellishment, its appendages – the ornamentation and illustration of the book in the change from roll to codex? What in the periods that followed was saved of the visual content of the rich stores of classical art? The answers to these questions must take three fundamental factors into account.

12
Papyrus fragment,
2nd century

The first is that in Antiquity only a very limited number of texts contained illustrations or indeed any kind of decoration, especially during the period of the papyrus roll. There were richly illustrated 'books' at that time, even real picture books, but they were a vanishing exception. In the process of changing from roll to codex, only a small selection of exemplars had illustrations or ornament which could be copied in the codex, or would find an equivalent there. Of the numerous papyri, fragments of rolls, found in Egypt, only very few are illustrated (fig. 12) or decorated; and not a single roll of classical origin, which might have included a pictorial sequence, or even a substantial fragment of such a roll, has come to light.[11] Of book painting in the Greek world, monopolized as it was by the papyrus roll, we can form only a very conjectural reconstruction.

This almost total vacuum makes it immensely difficult to estimate what the classical codex inherited pictorially from the papyrus roll. It is no longer generally accepted, for example, that any conclusions about the appearance of an antique illustrated roll can be drawn from the Middle Byzantine Joshua Roll in the Vatican (fig. 19), a post-classical roll. As a further complicating factor, only a very small number of illustrated classical codices on parchment – the direct successor to the illustrated roll – has survived (fig. 29); a few further examples are known through the efforts of Carolingian copyists (fig. 31), who had access to a larger number of classical manuscripts. Consequently, our knowledge of the decoration of the early parchment codex is severely limited.

The second factor to bear in mind on the question of the creative influence of the illustrated roll on book decoration, is the need for adjustment and modification brought about by the new format of the codex, a new medium, a changed spatial exercise. When columns of script were formed of short lines, as in the roll, the picture – in order to fit within the narrow frame determined by the width of the column – had to be concise: pictures in this context have an almost lapidary quality (fig. 7). But if the script area changes and the lines lengthen as in the codex, the space left free for the illustration within the framing script becomes much too broad for a picture inherited from a roll. Thus, if the model was copied without modification (for instance out of deference, which was not infrequently the case), then a literal, faithful reproduction of the original could not possibly fill the wide strips now created on the page, and empty gaps would result. From this discrepancy comes the impulse to devise filling motifs to plug these gaps, in other words to change the model.

Take a Carolingian Aratea manuscript, a copy of a classical manuscript: here the original picture is essentially retained but placed within the framing space of columns of script which have become much wider (fig. 13), with the effect of leaving the figures un-

13, 14
Signs of the Zodiac.
Computistical and astronomical
textbook. Metz, 820-840

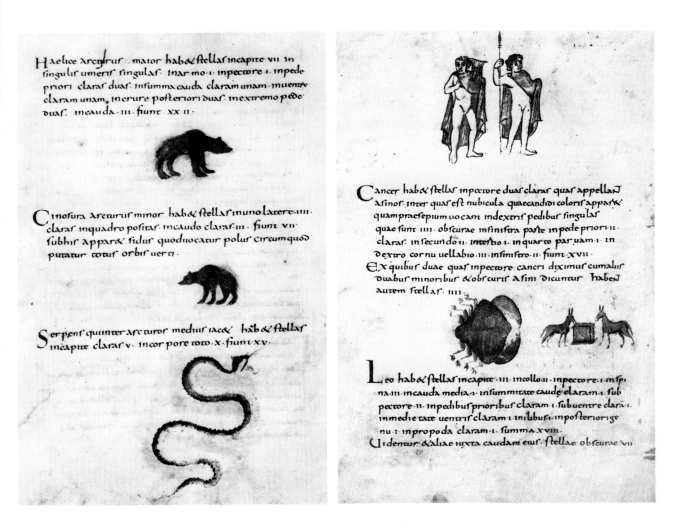

15
Psalm 41, 1:
The Hart drinking the Waters.
Stuttgart Psalter.
Saint-Germain-des-Prés (?),
first half of 9th century

anchored, floating in space. Another page from this manuscript (fig. 14) shows two illustrations pushed together side by side in one column in an attempt to solve the problem. If the pictorial element did not itself suffice to fill the space, a temptation arose to supplement the extant material, as one may see in the Stuttgart Psalter (fig. 15), although its prototype has not been clearly established. The example illustrates Psalm 41, 1 ... 'As the hart panteth for the cooling waters, so panteth my soul for Thee O Lord'. In the centre of the composition the hart drinks; on the right the Psalmist has come along to join in, and he gestures to the hand of God above and to the hart. This may well be the way in which an originally narrow composition would have been extended.

It would seem, therefore, that as far as the pictorial element is concerned, the assumption of absolute fidelity to the original will certainly create problems, and can no more be taken as an absolute fact than fidelity to the text itself. Alterations of text will inevitably occur through misreading and carelessness, and so we have textual corruption. Naturally, in the transmission of pictorial models corruption also occurs – meanings garbled because of a deficiency in the copyist's skill or a misunderstanding of the model. Even the most unadventurous copyist will always interpret his copy according to his preconceptions. Thus a *deliberate misunderstanding* resides in any new form, in the sense of 'having to speak in the language of one's own generation'. Any new interpretation is a translation into forms specifically intelligible and intended for one's contemporaries. This can be demonstrated by the juxtaposition of two examples: the first (fig. 16) is one of those numerous Byzantine Evangelist pictures which can still be recognized as deriving from late-classical author-portraits. The second is a northern, early-medieval copy of the subject (fig. 17).

16
St. John.
Byzantine Gospels.
Mid 10th century

17
St. Matthew.
Codex Millenarius.
Salzburg, c. 800

The philosophical posture of the two Evangelists – chin resting on hand – is the same. But note the changed shaft of the lectern. The copyist was understandably unfamiliar with the dolphin represented in his model. He translated it into a kind of dragon with sharp teeth, and curiously, with a decorative pattern around the eyes. When he gave it this particular shape, he doubtless thought he was improving it according to his own interpretation, drawing it more exactly. These are intentional 'improvements'; they arise from felt needs and conscious intentions[12], not from ineptitude. They are not signs of inferiority or lack of skill in the copyist.[13]

Yet even more important as an historical phenomenon is a second factor in the process of change and adaptation. Each type of 'book' appears to call forth from within not only pictorial formats suitable to its sole needs alone but also a system of decoration congenial solely to itself, and – most important – a form of narrative illustration intrinsic to itself. The continuous length of the roll of script, the 'locomotion' implicit in its format, the unrolling of it (which still echoes in the term 'volume' now applied to another referent), raised the possibility of creating laterally open pictorial compositions. The codex, with its sequence of relatively small, separate leaves, required

18
Lions.
Bestiary.
Peterborough (?),
early 13th century

22
Scenes from the Dacian wars.
Trajan's Column (detail).
Rome, early 2nd century

lateral enclosure of pictorial space, identifying it with the finite space of the page in the book (fig. 18).

Opinion is still divided over the interpretation of the pictorial sequences of the Vatican Joshua Roll (fig. 19). According to one view (Kurt Weitzmann),[14] it is a product of the Macedonian Renaissance of the tenth century, a sequence created from a number of originally separate single episodes; iconographically, its closest connection is to the illustrations of the slightly later Middle Byzantine Octateuch in the Vatican (figs. 20, 21). The other and older view (represented by Wickhoff)[15] is that the pictorial sequences were intrinsic to the roll format, rather like successive stills in a film. Certainly, this is a narrative structure – the continuous narrative story – with close affinities to the nature of the medium, the roll which unwinds a continuous text. Support for this concept is found in late-antique sculpture, for example, in the reliefs on the columns of Marcus Aurelius or Trajan (fig. 22) where the narrative spirals snake-like around the pillar. But if Weitzmann's thesis is correct, it means that the pictorial cycles of the Joshua Roll must be an artistic reconstruction from a classical picture-roll; however, no signs of continuous pictorial narratives appear in bona fide classical rolls, and therefore in the Joshua Roll we would be confronted with a historical phenomenon of the greatest rarity, that of a roll which devised, under the tutelage of some aca-

19
The Gibeonites before Joshua.
Joshua Roll.
Byzantine, 10th century

demic, a congenial narrative technique for its illustration – after the roll as a form had died out. This is a very difficult idea to accept.

Finally, a third factor must be taken into account before making any assessment of the epoch-making modification in the book format: the change from roll to codex coincided with a shift in intellectual outlook, in the values attached to experience of the physical world. Criteria based on perception were devalued, and this undoubtedly has the most intimate bearing on visual art. In the coastal regions of the eastern Mediterranean, the shift led, as is well known, to a positive hostility to figurative art.[16] Even in less extreme circumstances in the West, there was a growing inclination to regard external reality as a transient metaphor for the true, primary and invisible, transcendental world. A distinction began to be made between outward and inward looking. What was seen with the natural eye had only the value of a glassy reflection, a veiled intimation, a compass-needle pointing to something hidden behind the superficial surface of physical appearance – in short, as sign and symbol. If all things visible stood for

20, 21
The Gibeonites before Joshua.
Octateuch.
Byzantine, 11th century

something else, it follows that all pictorial art must become symbolic, a more or less abstract language of signs. As the pictorial language of art was suddenly perceived to be inwardly related to the sign language of the book, the barriers fell between two domains that had up to now been heterogeneous and in Antiquity fundamentally distinct. Wide perspectives opened up for a fruitful and creative interplay between word and picture, letter and figure, the arena of script and pictorial space. This symbiosis owes a great deal in its emergence and development to some of the most fertile displays of medieval artistic invention – the *figure initial,* in which the body of the letter was formed by a figure or figures (pl. XXX), the *historiated initial,* in which the interior of the letter was filled with figures or scenes (fig. 138); the *monogram page,* with script and ornament woven together in richly elaborated compositions (pl. III); the *drollery,* which claimed a free area of the page for the grotesque, for naturalistic graphics, genre scenes, etc. (figs. 23, 151); *didactic pictures,* with their penetrating fusion of pictorial and script elements in a manner impossible outside the book (fig. 166); *pictorial concordances,* like the 'Biblia pauperum' which by its juxtaposition of pictures points out their spiritual connection – prophecy and fulfilment (fig. 24),[17] and many others. These grew and flourished during the life-span of the illuminated book, and have no equivalent in the domain of monumental art, whether fresco, mosaic or panel painting.

What we have gained from the change from roll to codex – and in fact more so from its subsequent after-effects – is more easily evaluated than what we have lost: at that we can only guess. We can actually observe how new forms and means of expression continuously emerge from the unprecedented co-existence of script, picture and ornament; but no archaeologist's spade can uncover the pictorial cycles that perished with the destruction of illustrated rolls where not even

23
Drollery.
Robert de Boron,
L'Histoire du Graal.
Northern France, c. 1280

24
Christ carrying the Cross,
with two typological scenes.
Biblia pauperum.
Block book. Dutch, c. 1430–1440

fragments remain. How enormous this loss must have been, can be seen in the illustration of the Bible, a tradition which was never completely abandoned despite change of medium, cultural catastrophe and artistic crisis. The oldest biblical cycles, which were certainly designed for illustrated rolls, fed the whole of early medieval Bible illustration, including the Romanesque. Extracts from the original pictorial sequences were made in Early Christian codices; and later, again in excerpts and in ever dwindling numbers, they were used right up to the late Middle Ages. In the Vienna Genesis (pl. I), a 'Purpurcodex' (book on purple parchment) made for a Byzantine emperor, we have an early example of this reduction: a sequence of pictures from Genesis in a still richly illustrated fragment of 48 pages (from an original of at least 200 pages). Carolingian Bibles condensed the illustration of a single book – often only of Genesis – into the frontispiece, as pictorial strips confined to one side of the page (pl. XI);

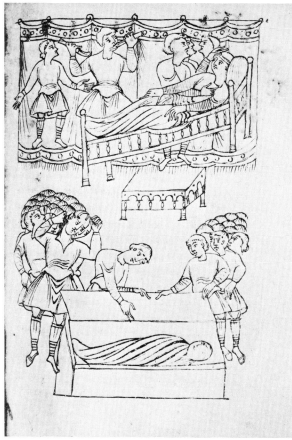

and these, where their iconographical sources or analogies can be easily identified, may be regarded as extracts from infinitely richer cycles. Taking an example from the illustrations for the Book of Maccabees, let me briefly indicate how this gradual reduction took place, and how the stream of pictorial material became thinner and thinner, trickling finally into a few mere frontispieces. We have a late-Carolingian manuscript, probably from St. Gall, in which a sequence of twenty-six separate pictorial pages recounts the history of the Maccabees (figs. 25, 26). There is no doubt that this Carolingian sequence is only a copy of a late-antique model. In two Bibles of the Romanesque period, one from Cîteaux and the other from Winchester, it is precisely the Book of Maccabees that is given illustrated title-pages (figs. 27, 28). The sequence of scenes, arranged in several rows, one upon another, bears close parallels to the St. Gall cycle: for example, to take only two details, in the gestures of the mourners in each case; in the last episodes (Death of Judas Maccabeus): or in the arrangement of the composition's pictorial space which is cut off sharply at the sides (St. Gall and Winchester).

If we pursue the history of this tradition, we inevitably come to the conclusion that by far the richest and most detailed Bible picture-cycles came at the beginning of that tradition; indeed, that the biblical text was later on never again so thoroughly and completely illustrated.

25
King Antiochus
issuing commands.
Book of Maccabees.
St. Gall,
first half of 10th century

26
Death of Judas Maccabeus.
Book of Maccabees.
St. Gall,
first half of 10th century

This at any rate is true of the Old Testament; there is no trace to be found of early cyclical representations of the Gospels. What this discrepancy signified was for a long time puzzling. The presence of numerous apocryphal Jewish elements in the Old Testament cycles, however, indicated to those who studied the problem a plausible explanation: the Old Testament pictorial cycles had to be of pre-Christian origin, when the Jewish community, under Hellenistic influence, did not observe their ban on pictorial art. That would imply, however – and this is for us the decisive factor – that these cycles originated at a time when the codex did not yet exist. In a word: the narrative cycle, which is not the same thing as continuous narrative, is in fact the legacy of classical roll-illustration to medieval book-illumination. And it sufficed, as we have seen, in the further course of medieval development, for fragmentary copies of such pictorial cycles to find their way into the hands of illuminators at a suitable moment, to resuscitate cyclical illustration. It enabled narrative art eventually to rise reborn, like the phoenix from the ashes – a superb example of the immortality of artistic ideas.

27
Death of Judas Maccabeus.
Bible of Stephen Harding.
Cîteaux, early 12th century

28
King Antiochus
issuing commands;
death of Judas Maccabeus.
Winchester Bible.
Winchester, c. 1150-1180

I · Pictorial Decoration
in the Organic Structure of the Book

ONE OF THE BASIC requirements for an understanding of medieval illumination is to have a clear idea of how the miniature or pictorial decoration is anchored in the organic structure of the book, both physically and conceptually. There is little hope of grasping the artistic meaning of a medieval or a baroque altarpiece, or the jamb-figures on a cathedral portal, if they are studied as isolated museum pieces with no account of how they function in sacral space or how they are related to similar examples around them. In the same way, to attempt to understand a miniature out of context is to commit an act of intellectual vandalism akin to that of zealous art lovers who, over the centuries, actually cut initials or miniatures out of manuscripts in order to hang them neatly on the wall in picture-frames, giving a false identity to the fragments.

The best and quickest way of grasping the peculiar nature of the art of illumination is to consider the practical experience of anyone who studies illuminated manuscripts for the first time. The great surprise for an attentive novice is that, having looked through a few

29
Ascanius's council of war.
Vatican Virgil.
Italy (?), early 5th century

manuscript collections, he or she finds that there were always only relatively few texts which were illustrated or even decorated, except in the late medieval period; and further, that there are only a few fixed places in the book where such embellishment occurs and that, in fact, it always differs according to the text in question. Even in Antiquity, as far as can be judged from the fragmented records, only certain works seem to have provided an occasion for illustration. There is no apparent explanation for this. It is certainly not due to any accident of preservation that we know of various illustrated Virgils (fig. 29) but can uncover no trace of an illustrated Ovid. Late medieval illustrations of the Christian moralized Ovid are not based on any classical pictorial tradition; they are direct textual illustrations, which seem to us rather naïve, pictorial translations of verbal details and descriptions; for example, the panther of Bacchus is represented in a Flemish miniature as a hybrid monster with the torso of a griffin and the hind-quarters of a lion (fig. 30). That we have illustrations of Terence (fig. 31) but none of Plautus, the other great Roman comedian, is as baffling as the absence of a tradition of Ovid illustration. To us it remains incomprehensible that such a subject as that of Ovid's Metamorphoses, which the Renaissance made so much of, inspired no pictorial representation of the text in earlier times.

The Middle Ages adopted a completely passive attitude towards the pictorial tradition of classical texts right up to the Gothic. The pictorial element in the works of classical authors was not infrequently appropriated and in the process adapted and paraphrased. But, as far as we know, never, until the Gothic period, did medieval artists voluntarily provide a classical text with pictures where none were supplied.

30
Bacchus.
Ovid moralisé.
Flanders, c. 1480

31
Illustration to Andria,
Act II, Scene 6. Terence, Comedies.
Reims, second half of 9th century

32
Clerics singing psalms.
Ivory, late Carolingian

33
Celebration of the Mass.
Ivory, late 10th century

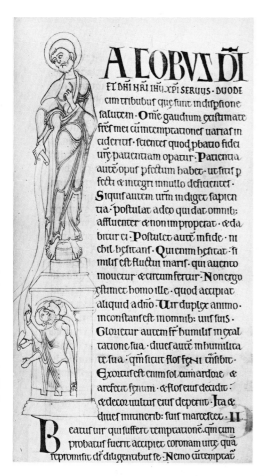

34
Jacob.
Winchester Bible.
Winchester, c. 1150–1180

We shall understand the relationship better in the context of Christian literature. In the early period, it was almost exclusively the books used in Church services which received artistic decoration: the Sacramentary, later known as the Missal, the Gospel Book and Gospel Lectionary, the Psalter, the Pontifical and the Benedictional, and in later centuries, the choir books – compilations of texts of the chant. Two ivories of the late-Carolingian School, probably from Lorraine, depicting scenes from the liturgy, show the books in use. In one (fig. 32), a priest, surrounded by singing monks and in the foreground a deacon, holds an open book in his left hand. We can even read the words written on its pages: 'Ad te Domine levavi animam meam', the beginning of Psalm 24; it is therefore a Psalter. In the second ivory (fig. 33), the priest, again surrounded by monks and deacons, appears only as a half-figure; in those days the priest stood behind the altar. The book before him is open at the Canon of the Mass, and on it we can read the words which he speaks immediately before the Eucharistic Sacrifice: 'Te igitur clementissime pater ...'; therefore, the book is a Sacramentary (the closed book at the other side of the altar must then be a Gospel Book). Psalter, Gospels, Sacramentary – not the Bible – these are the principal books to be illustrated in the early period of the Middle Ages. The Bible itself, the collection of all the texts which make up the Holy Scripture was at that time, for reasons already given, not regarded as an object suitable for pictorial or decorative embellishment. The Ottonian period for example, so fond of illustration, apparently produced no illustrated Bible.

However, the situation changed abruptly in the twelfth century, when medieval Bible decoration and illustration reached its zenith. Very likely the great monastic reforms effected this change by stipulating reading of the Bible in refectory and laying emphasis on more accurate redactions of the text. An English chronicle refers to a very beautiful Bible which was used at Winchester for reading during meal times,[18] and this is probably the same *de luxe* book still to be found in Winchester Cathedral (pl. XXIII). The important thing is that at that time the Bible was raised from a merely academic existence and given a specific, practical function, not in Church usage but still as part of official monastic life. In the Winchester Bible (fig. 34) we find initials that have been sketched but not finished; in the accompanying text, we observe abbreviation signs, notations of rising and falling inflexion to help in reading the text aloud. In general, it can be said that the more private the character of a text or book, the less the incentive to provide decoration.

Thus, at least until the Romanesque period, the principal artistic development was essentially to be found in those liturgical books already mentioned. And equally clearly, it was liturgical use that determined the artistic organization of the book, the Sacramentary, Psalter or Lectionary. To find the decorated pages one would have to turn to a different place in each case. If it is a Gospel Book, or rather one of the four versions of the Life of Christ sanctioned by the Church (what is known in Greek as a Tetraevangeliary) then one can expect to find a kind of frontispiece at the beginning of each Gospel. this takes the form of an author-portrait (pls. V, VI) or an Evangelist symbol (pl. II)[19] or a combination of the two. When symbol and Evangelist are combined, they can be on facing pages (fig. 35), or on the same page – with the symbol used as filling of the lunette of a quasi-architectural frame (fig. 36) or with the Evangelist and his symbol placed together in the same pictorial space (fig. 181), an arrangement which becomes the norm in the later Middle Ages.[20] In a Sacramentary or Missal, however, from the Carolingian period onwards, one will look in vain for a frontispiece; the principal and often the only decoration will be found in the most important section of the text, the Canon of the Mass, which contains the consecratory prayer at the Sacrifice. And indeed, two places in the Canon are regularly distinguished by pictorial or even simply ornamental embellishment – the beginning of the Preface (pl. XVI, figs. 40, 105) and the beginning of the Canon proper (pl. XVII, figs. 39, 106).

It may be useful to say a word about the difference between Sacramentary and Missal. The ceremony of the Mass was enacted in diverse roles: prayers, lessons and chant fell to different participants. The Sacramentary contained only the prayers, that is to say the part which the priest himself celebrated (fig. 33). It was not until the tenth century that the first complete Missal appeared, or to be more precise, gradually evolved as a collective text which contained the other parts necessary for the celebration of the Mass. The Liber sacramentorum (Sacramentary) was arranged in the calendrical sequence, and in Carolingian times, the text of the Canon, that is of the Eucharistic prayers,

35
St. Luke and his symbol.
Codex Millenarius.
Salzburg, c. 800

36
St. Luke with his symbol,
and scenes from the Life of Christ.
Gospels of St. Augustine.
Italian, 6th century

stood at the beginning of the book; later, from the eleventh century, however, the Canon was moved back to the middle, to where the codex most easily fell open, and found there the position it has continued to occupy – before Easter Mass, the most important feast in the Church calendar.

The most characteristic decoration of the Sacramentary, namely that which concentrates on honouring the Prefatio communis and the Canon, first appears in the Carolingian period. Mass books of pre-Carolingian date, in other words those of the Merovingians, in which Preface and Canon usually come at the end of the book (a good example is the Gelasian Sacramentary), left these important sections almost entirely undecorated; they supplied only the three major divisions of the book with frontispieces, using material not essentially different from that of other liturgical books since Early Christian times – arcades or the Cross (fig. 37). The beginning of the text of the Canon proper, 'Te Igitur ...', which was to have such a magnificent future in book ornamentation (fig. 39) finds itself swamped in the middle of a page, in the middle of a line, without any emphasis, in early examples (fig. 38).

37
Incipit
to the second major division
of the Gelasian Sacramentary.
France, c. 750

Towards the end of the eighth century, in 789, Pope Hadrian I sent Charlemagne, at his request, a Sacramentary allegedly in the form edited by Gregory the Great and thus of the sixth century. Charlemagne recommended it to the Frankish Church as a model. In contrast to the Merovingian Sacramentary, the Canon of this exemplar occupied the beginning, not the end, of the book, and that may have inspired artist and scribe to put the primary visual emphasis on the centrepiece of the Mass which had moved, so to speak, into the foreground. A ligature formed the starting point of the design: the intertwined letters of V and D, of the words 'Vere dignum … et iustum est, aequum et salutare, nos tibi semper, et ubique gratias agere', words which, because of their frequent repetition, had for a long time already been abbreviated by scribes to VD. Often the scribe let the stroke of abbreviation cross the intersecting capitals, and this was how the established formula of the Vere-Dignum sign originated (fig. 41), a monogram in the nature of the Christogram and the basis of all future decoration, ornamental and figural.

It is typical of the medieval process that, out of the simple paraphrase represented by this sign, a pictorial form emerges, pregnant

38
Text page with the Canon of the Mass.
Gelasian Sacramentary.
France, c. 750

39
'Te' monogram
preceding the Canon of the Mass.
Sacramentary fragment.
Northern France, c. 860

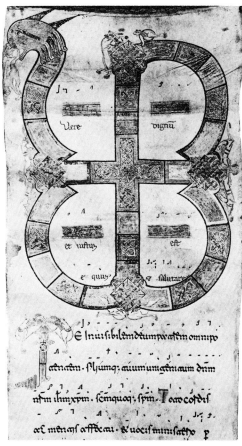

with meaning, until at last the abstract physiognomy of this symbolic form is replaced by a concrete one – a revelation made flesh as the figure of the living God is conjured up. The *Majestas Domini* is here represented, to whom are addressed the words immediately following 'Vere dignum ... Domine sancte, Pater omnipotens ...' (fig. 42).[21] In the transitional stage, Christ in Majesty appears either as a medallion-filling in the intersection of the Preface initial, partial (head or bust) or entire figure (as in the example just given), or independently alongside the letter as a purely external addition (fig. 43). The latter was especially characteristic of later Italian art where there was far less understanding of the peculiar medieval intermingling of sign and picture than there was in northern art. At the end of this development, the *Majestas Domini* became the typical picture preceding the Canon of the Mass (fig. 44). This *transition from sign to picture,* which touches the very nerve centre of artistic creation in the field of illumination, will be examined in greater detail when we look at the second principal element in the decoration of the Sacramentary – the opening phrase of the Canon proper. This begins with the words, 'Te igitur clementissime Pater, per Jesum Christum Filium tuum Dominum nostrum, supplices rogamus, ac petimus ...'; and it was inevitable that the first letter, the T, as an initial, would be of larger format and emphasized by ornament, that it would interact with the letters that

40
Preface monogram.
Sacramentary fragment.
Northern France, c. 860

41
Preface monogram.
Exultet Roll.
Montecassino, mid 11th century

42
Christ in Majesty,
opening to the Preface.
Exultet Roll.
Benevento, 12th century

43
Christ in Majesty,
opening to the Preface.
Sacramentary.
Tuscany, c. 1100

44
Christ in Majesty,
opening to the Preface.
Missal. St. Florian,
c. 1305–1310

follow, and would be fused into an elaborately patterned monogram (fig. 45). The T (Greek Tau), however, charged with meaning since Early Christian times, was automatically understood as a symbol of the Cross and the Crucified Christ. For the medieval imagination, it was the most natural thing in the world to change an abstract geometrical sign into an anthropomorphic form. One of the earliest surviving Sacramentaries, from Gellone (late eighth century), already offers the Crucified Christ at this point in the Mass (fig. 46); and so here word becomes picture. This occurred in advance of the general development, in an artistic environment in which there was continual experimentation with initials transformed as figures or even disguised as figures. The Tau-Cross of the Sacramentary of Gellone, however, remained for some time an isolated exception.

Equating T with the Crucified Christ came into current use in Sacramentary decoration only in the Ottonian period (pl. XVII),[22] a time when the urge for pictorial expression was overpowering and when every opportunity for experimenting with form was seized. Yet at the same time magnificent non-figural initials were created, as expressive as representational treatments of the most significant religious themes. And so we find, in most Ottonian Sacramentaries, a purely ornamental Preface sign coupled with a pictorial Te Igitur (pls. XVI, XVII). In the Romanesque period, the tendency to use pictorial versions in both ornamental positions in the Sacramentary became

45
'Te' monogram
preceding the Canon of the Mass.
'Missal' of Robert of Jumièges.
Canterbury, c. 1020

46
Initial T as Crucifixion
preceding the Canon of the Mass.
Gellone Sacramentary,
c. 790-795

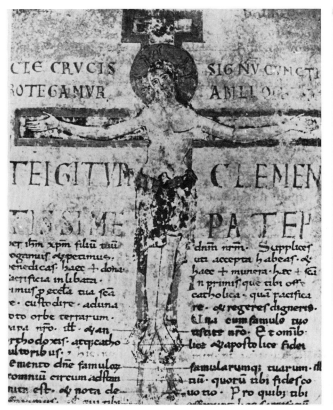

47
Initial T as Crucifixion
preceding the Canon of the Mass.
Sacramentary.
Tuscany, c. 1100

48
Crucifixion
preceding the Canon of the Mass.
Walling Missal.
St. Florian, c. 1310

notably stronger (figs. 43, 47); in the Gothic period, the Gothic Missal – which had replaced the Sacramentary – used only the Canon *picture* (fig. 48), the Crucifixion, alone or paired with Christ in Majesty which had evolved before it. In the history and genealogy of the Canon *picture,* a good many of the aspirations, efforts and fortunes of the whole of medieval illumination are reflected.

This particular example is of special interest because we know from contemporary commentaries how it was regarded. Pope Innocent III, who died in 1216, gave the following explanation of the Canon of the Mass: the believer is meant to be reminded of the Passion and therefore in some Sacramentaries the image of Christ would be found between Preface and Canon, 'ut non solum intellectus litterae, verum etiam aspectus picturae memoriam passionis Domini inspiret', so that not only the understanding of the word but also the sight of the picture may inspire remembrance, the 'memoria' of the Passion of the Lord. In this commentary, the function of pictorial representation was obviously understood as a means of becoming inwardly aware, as well as of visualizing. And Innocent continued, 'Et forte divina factum est providentia, ut ab ea littera T [Tau] canon inciperet, quae sui forma signum crucis ostendit et exprimit in figura', 'and it is a happy chance of Divine Providence that the Canon begins with that letter T [Tau], which shows in its shape the sign of the Cross and expresses it figurally'.[23] We see that Pope Innocent was himself well aware of the initial's two-fold character, the interchangeability of the letter and the picture; and we may recall at the same time that the priest celebrating the Mass by the gesture of his outstretched arm, in turn, again evokes the imagery of the figure of the Cross, and further, that in the Mass, the consecration of the bloodless Sacrifice of bread and wine is a symbolic representation of the Sacrifice of the Cross.

Here, if I may be permitted a short excursus, it should not be forgotten that clerical commentaries on the significance of the Preface sign exist, if not from the early, at least from the later Middle Ages (pl. XVI). A twelfth-century text, the 'Rationale divini officii' by John Beleth, Rector of Paris University, gives the following description of the Preface sign: 'One finds (he says) at this point (in the Missal), a 'figura' (in other words, a pattern), which is like our Delta or D, wholly enclosed; in the foreground there is an outline of a V [U], open at the top; the middle is crossed by a horizontal stroke which joins both these in the manner of a cross'. Then follows the exegesis characteristic of a medieval theologian: 'Quod quidem non sine causa factum est' – 'This is not without deeper meaning': Delta, enclosed on all sides, signifies Divine Nature, which has neither beginning nor end; V stands for Christ's human nature which originated in the Virgin but is without end. The hyphen in the middle, however, which links the two parts, is the Cross, signifying the tie between mankind and God.[24] A century later, Guilielmus Durandus in his 'Rationale', a fundamental text for the later Middle Ages, repeated the same interpretation more elaborately: '[The letters are placed at the beginning of the Preface] because through the mystery of [this] union, both shall men be reconciled to angels through the Lord's Passion, and the human be joined with the divine in praise of the Saviour'.[25] These interpretations are quoted not because I believe them to be conclusive; on the contrary, they are examples of inductive logic, of mystical allegorical interpretation which subordinates meaning and motive and plays no part in the genesis of the pattern in question. These examples, which could almost be called theological word games, tell us much about the intellectual habit of moralizing but nothing about the essence of the work they interpret. I mention them nonetheless, because unfortunately allegorical exegesis has become very fashionable again in art history, despite the fact that it obscures those paths which lead to a true understanding of the historical monuments. The symbolism of Te Igitur can be experienced directly; the symbolism upon which the Preface sign is supposedly based is the speculative projection of theologians.

II · The Initial

IN DISCUSSING the decoration of the Sacramentary, we touched upon a phenomenon uniquely characteristic of the illuminated book – the interplay of script, decoration and picture. From this interrelationship the initial as a creative form was born, its meaning and justification wholly prescribed by the art of illumination. Antiquity can claim invention of the initial (fig. 51), but it was in the Middle Ages that it first became a fruitful formal motif for the artistic imagination. Both practical and aesthetic factors were significant in the actual origin of the initial, but the aesthetic soon triumphed and the initial thus came to occupy an autonomous sphere midway between script and picture.

Already in Antiquity it was considered a practical necessity to give some visual indication of the beginning of a paragraph or entry; and this was done by marking the point either by a small hyphen, the 'paragraphos', inserted between the lines, or by a simple tick, the 'koronis' (fig. 49). It must be remembered that classical script had neither separation of words nor internal punctuation, although these distinctions were introduced towards the end of the period; thus a line was written continuously without spacing. As a result, it was not easy to see the interpolated paragraph signs. It is difficult to understand today how the classical reader put up with a continuous script so different from speech. We ought to consider, however, that in Antiquity there must have been great reluctance to break up the wall of script and to leave empty spaces of the sort one expects at the beginning and end of sections. Incidentally, paragraph signs were originally understood only as terminating marks, that is, as signalling the end of a text rather than mark its beginning.

From a desire to make subdivisions more distinct, the first letter began to be moved out into the margin (even when it did not begin

50
Text page.
Codex Alexandrinus,
first half of 5th century

a new paragraph) and it was soon distinguished by larger format and decoration, as seen, for instance, in the Codex Alexandrinus (fig. 50), which illustrates the early practice of giving the title of a work at the end of the text (First Epistle to the Romans). In these modest markers, we have the embryo of the prodigious development of the post-classical initial. We know very little about the classical initial itself before the fourth century, when the codex became the principal form of book. A Vatican Virgil manuscript of the fifth century already has fully formed initials (fig. 51), divorced in every respect from the rest of the script. There are no examples of so early a date in eastern manuscripts. The paucity of examples in early Greek codices does not, however, mean that the decorated initial originated in the Latin West. On the contrary, in the Greek East the initial appears originally to have developed from the decoration of the last page of text, the Explicit page, as a consequence of emphasizing the page that contained the title of the work, as in the example of fig. 9, 'Evangelion kata joannem'. The future in book decoration, however, lay in emphasizing the beginning of the text, the head of the book, as indeed subsequent developments proved. An indication of such a changing trend

51
Text page (detail).
Vergilius Augusteus.
Roman, 5th century

can be seen in the Valerianus Gospels which combines Explicit and Incipit (fig. 52): 'Secundum Iohannem explicit Amen. Incipit secundum Lukam.'

It is further important to note that the ornamental vocabulary used in the earliest initials, Italian as well as Gallic, is zoomorphic – the familiar fish/bird design (fig. 53, cf. fig. 37), whose origins and early symbolism remain obscure. It has still not been proved that the fish motif enjoyed such great popularity because it had a Eucharistic significance, nor has it been clarified whether the fish/bird motif of late-classical and Merovingian initials is connected directly to the

52
Explicit-Incipit.
Gospels of St. John and St. Luke.
Valerian Gospels.
North-eastern Italy, c. 675

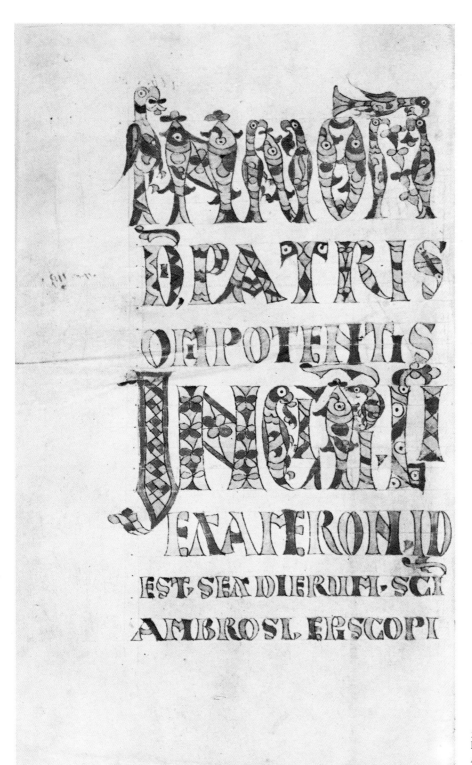

IN
D PATRIS
OMPOTENTIS
INCPT
EXAMERON ID
EST SEX DIERVM · SCI
AMBROSI EPSCOPI

53
Incipit.
Ambrose, Hexameron.
Corbie, second half of 8th century

54
Incipit.
St. Luke's Gospel.
Book of Kells.
Insular, after 800

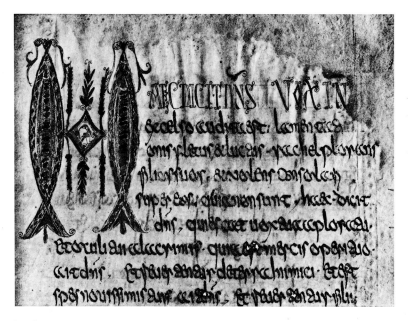

55
Initial, Lectionary from Luxeuil.
Luxeuil, 7th-8th century

oriental zoomorphic initial found in Armenian manuscripts.[26]
Strzygowski was the first to suspect a common origin,[27] and postula-
ted an Eastern source. But Armenian examples are no earlier than
the tenth century, and zoomorphic initials in Hebraic manuscripts[28]
could be cited from much earlier. The riddle of these analogies has
not yet been solved.

Nevertheless, we may conclude that the combination and intermingling of abstract signs and organic forms (or of ornament derived from
organic form) is not a classical concept; on the contrary, whenever we
glimpse classical tradition in the Middle Ages, we see a rigorously
maintained division between script and picture. It is probably correct
to view the polymorphic initial structure of medieval illumination as
an anti-classical element in the texture of medieval art.

55a
Initials.
Gospel Lectionary from Chelles,
c. 800

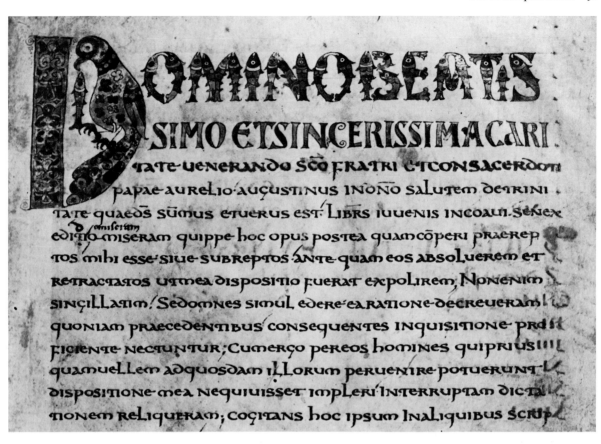

56
Incipit.
St. Augustine, *De Trinitate*.
Northern France, mid 8th century

57
Detail of fig. 53

A letter is a sign, an unambiguous element, meant to be understood in one way and not in another. If a letter is replaced by forms which suggest or at least refer to some external reality, there is the risk that the alphabet will be rendered illegible. The initial, which was invented to increase legibility of text (as in the Incipit-initials pushed out into the margin), reversed its own impetus and unleashed a flood of indecipherable decorations, engulfing its natural alphabetical form. A climax in this development can without doubt be seen in the Book of Kells (fig. 54).

The art of the medieval illuminator lay precisely in this transformation of one thing into another – of a letter into the body of a fish (figs. 55, 55a) or a human figure into a letter (fig. 34), just as it was the business of a medieval mason to transform a human figure into a pillar (fig. 156) or a rain-spout into a lively gargoyle.

The simplest form of transformation was that of substituting heterogeneous elements for the various parts of the letter – shafts, bows, replaced by zoomorphic motifs (fig. 56). The initials of different pre-Carolingian schools of the Frankish empire were constructed according to this principle, but in the process the zoomorphic forms were completely divested of organic life and changed into symbolic abstractions. Even animal forms were broken down into their components to fit better into geometrical forms (fig. 57).

The eighth century did not stop at assembling letters in verticals, diagonals and curves, like matchsticks; in the later part of this development, it attempted to restore a measure of organic life to animal forms and created a new relationship between the structure of the letter and its zoomorphic elements: animal forms cease to be merely units and begin to play an active role in the composition of the letter. In the movement of living creatures, their bending and stretching, the body of the letter is created (fig. 58). These examples confront us with the creation of structure as a living process.

Admittedly, there is no naturalistic life in these initials, only an imaginative simulation of organic movement. These living creatures – the fauna of a zoomorphic vocabulary seem to have grown considerably in number and include quadrupeds – now have command over every kind of acrobatic movement (fig. 59), so they can easily conjure up any required shape of letter by appropriate contortions. This dynamism has a further dimension – one natural species can be changed into another in fluent transition. A fish suddenly becomes a quadruped; a plant ends in an animal head rather than in a flower; an organic form becomes inorganic. In the fish/bird initial, zoomorphic elements were added one by one; now there is a continual change of individual forms of nature. The representation of a hound suckling her young in a D-initial (fig. 60) at first works entirely naturalistically; however, if you follow the tail of the animal, it suddenly becomes something else – the extension of a dragon-like beast, which in turn becomes an interlace ornament, ending in a shaft which passes through the muzzle of the hound. The principle at work in the composition of this initial is *kaleidoscopic metamorphosis,* a configurative shift-shaping

58
Figure initial:
fox and raven.
Canonical writings.
Corbie, 8th century

59
Zoomorphic initial.
St. Augustine,
Quaestiones in Heptateuchon.
Northern France, mid 8th century

60, 61
Figure initials:
hound suckling her young;
Habakkuk's thanksgiving.
Corbie Psalter.
Corbie, c. 800

62
Figure initial:
Jonah and the whale.
Corbie Psalter.
Corbie, c. 800

which comprehends essentially one moment in time, however unreal. In reading this type of initial, we participate in its self-creation almost as if being told a story.

In one of these initials (fig. 61), we trace a horse's tail as it changes into the hull of a ship, and the prow of the boat as it becomes in turn the tip of a Phrygian cap of the helmsman who sits in the boat and seemingly guides it. And finally, this is no longer a boat but a kind of wagon on wheels. Usually such a composition would be classified as a figure initial, but this could almost be called an historiated one, except that in the usual historiated initial the letter forms the frame for the scene represented; here, the letter and the scene are one. Another initial from the same manuscript tells the story of Jonah and the whale as follows (fig. 62): the boat from which Jonah is cast into the sea changes abruptly into the tail of the sea-monster whose gaping mouth receives the prophet. And because Jonah's legs appear to develop directly from the ship's prow and to continue it, the whole composition forms a kind of figure-of-eight and a continuous recycling structure. The dream of perpetual motion appears to have been achieved – the form of the letter is never completed; it disappears and is recreated forever.

These two initials and many more decorate a Psalter which was written shortly after 800 A.D. for the monastery of Corbie in Picardy (northern France). Though executed in Carolingian times, its decoration is decidedly pre-Carolingian. In Carolingian illumination proper and the subsequent Ottonian period, zoomorphic initials are rare; a decided effort was made to adhere to classical standards in decorative as well as figurative subjects, and that meant a kind of monopoly

63
Initial. Gospels.
Schools of Tours,
mid 9th century

64
Fragment of Irish stone cross
with animal interlace.
Aberlady, East Lothian, c. 800

for classical acanthus ornament. It also meant, however, and most importantly, that boundaries between ornament and script remained firmly intact: the stem of the initial may have been decorated with a filling of vine tendrils, botanical ornaments at the ends of the shaft or at its angles, but the clear geometrical form of the letter is not obscured (fig. 63).

The history of what we may call kaleidoscopic structuring of the initial was, however, by no means at an end; centuries later, in the Romanesque period, the original goals of pre-Carolingian illuminators, stifled by the Renaissance that Charlemagne had engineered and supervised, amazingly acquired new life. Deep-rooted links connect pre-Carolingian and Romanesque art – for example, the animal ornament and animal interlace of Insular art (fig. 64) and the beast-columns of Romanesque sculpture (fig. 65); and in the case of the initial, there is also a direct reference back to compositions pioneered by pre-Carolingians (cf. figs. 66, 67).

65
Trumeau (detail).
Souillac, southern France,
second quarter of 12th century

A figure initial, from a Gospel Book now in the Cathedral Treasury at Essen (fig. 68), will illustrate this resurgence of pre-Carolingian ideas in illumination. The illuminator, if not a contemporary of, was at least closely akin in sensibility to the Corbie Master. His L-initial has obviously developed from the zoomorphic initial: a beast of prey, pursuing a small quadruped, abruptly changes the direction of its body, switching from the horizontal into the vertical plane, and balancing on its nose a winged biped whose outstretched body forms the top part of the ascender of the L. In earlier examples of pre-Carolingian illumination, single zoomorphic creatures were used as equivalents of units in the structure of the letter. In the Essen Gospels, there is a different approach. The position of the joints of the animal and its physiognomy are not correlated to the anatomy and structure of the letter. A change in direction and movement of the animal begets the right-angled orientation characteristic of the letter L.

66
Figure initial.
Corbie Psalter.
Corbie, c. 800

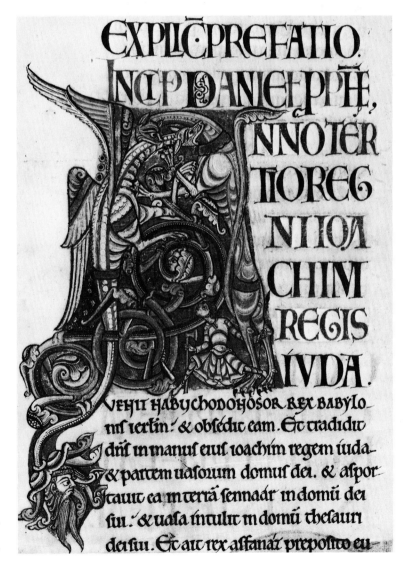

67
Initial to the Book of Daniel.
Bible. Winchester, mid 12th century

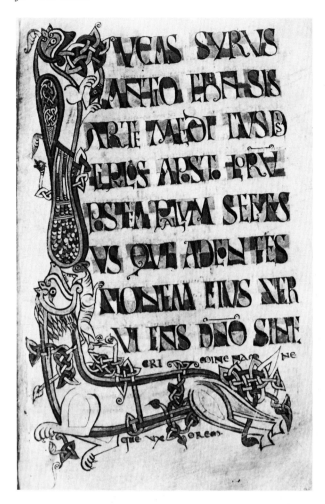

68
Initial L.
Gospels, 8th century

Three-hundred and fifty years later, the imagination of an English illuminator was caught by the same idea and he created an L-initial which uses almost the same formal elements (fig. 69). Admittedly, in the intervening years a botanical vocabulary of ornament had provided the basis for the construction of initials, and it could not be wholly displaced, not even by the zoomorphic ornament retrospectively adopted from pre-Carolingian initial patterns. In Romanesque initials, the quadruped and biped animals which the beast of prey pursued in pre-Carolingian initials have vanished. And precisely how the relationship between animal and plant should be interpreted is not clear. Is the beast of prey devouring the vegetation or does it sprout from the animal's jaws? According to everything we know about medieval inventiveness, this possibility of diverse or ambiguous interpretation was as a rule thoroughly desirable, if not actively sought.

Ambivalence of form is therefore an inescapable prerequisite of kaleidoscopic construction. The medieval artist and his public, if not religious zealots or purists like St. Bernard, must have taken special delight in seeing the dynamic upward thrust of an animal suddenly

69
Initial to the Book of Numbers.
Bible. Winchester, mid 12th century

change into the burgeoning spume of a flowering plant, whose cascading foliage again reverses the direction of the movement. These reversals of movement accompany a second metamorphosis: from zoomorphic to botanic form, and then from the recesses of the lowermost leaves, anthropomorphic human heads suddenly peer forth. Finally, by ingenious interweaving of motifs and direction of movement in such compositions there is created a kind of equipoise between the two kinds of organic life. A notable aspect of the phenomenon is how objective representation is transformed into abstract ornament and reconverted into the former. Needless to say, this special case is of the greatest importance for the interrelationship between letter and picture – a continous conflict for over a thousand years – whether the design is ornamental or figurative.

Parallel to the kaleidoscopic initial and from almost the same regions and the same period, we find the specifically anthropomorphic, purely figural initial. The enlivened stems, crossbars and bows of the Corbie Psalter initials enact complete scenes – David and Goliath (fig. 70), the Presentation in the Temple (fig. 71), the Annunciation (fig. 72) – probably the only Annunciation in the history of art to have two Marys since the illuminator needed them to construct the M of the Magnificat (Luke I., 47-55). For a hundred years there was little development in the figure initial until around the turn of the eleventh and the twelfth century, when the concept again excited the artistic imagination and produced congenial successors to the Corbie Master in the illuminators from Cîteaux in Burgundy. The artist who executed a large Bible and Gregory's *Moralia in Job,* both works in several volumes (the enterprise devised and guided by the artistically-minded Abbot Stephen Harding), brought the composition of the figure initial to its peak. Instead of trying to adjust a given form of letter to a similarly prescribed iconographic motif such as the Presentation (fig. 71), he confined himself to interpreting the structure of letters in

70-72
Figure initials:
David and Goliath;
Presentation in the Temple;
Annunciation.
Corbie Psalter.
Corbie, c. 800

73-75
Figure initials:
monks chopping wood;
horse and fallen rider;
falconer and waterfowl.
Gregory, Moralia in Job.
Cîteaux, early 12th century

terms of scenes from daily monastic life and personal experience. A pair of monks chopping wood form a Q (fig. 73) in which their backs bend along the curve of the letter and add a humorous touch to the composition. Or the stem of an I (pl. XXII) is changed into a tree-trunk, at the foot of which one monk wields an axe while the other prunes the crown. This represents a literal 'landscaping' of the initial, a 'naturalizing' – when, for instance, the tail of a Q (fig. 75) flows out as water in which waterfowl jostle, while a falconer moves across the outline of the letter; or when a horse throws its rider who falls outside the circle of the initial to form the tail of the Q (fig. 74).

At the same time, the Masters of Cîteaux were enriching their imagination with yet another concept of form that derives from the pagan, insular, legacy to medieval art: the idea of an endless entwining

76
Carpet page.
Book of Durrow.
Insular, c. 680

77
Beast column.
Souillac, southern France,
second quarter of 12th century

of form, first manifested in northern animal ornament (fig. 76) with
its nightmare of writhing organic life, linked by clenched teeth each
to the other, interpenetrating one another in a mortal struggle for
existence. A war of all against all with aggression directed even against
the aggressor's own body, which admittedly does not remain a body
but is denatured to ribbon-work. In this vehement entanglement of
forms, any free space is eliminated. Indeed, it is exactly this loss of
space which gives the composition its characteristic terrifying force –
of ensnared creatures locked in hopeless and inescapable struggle.
Now suddenly, in the Romanesque period, after several centuries,

the pagan concepts of interweaving re-appear both in monumental sculpture and in illuminated manuscripts. If in sculpture we refer to a beast-column, the most ingenious examples of which come from southern France, Moissac and Souillac (fig. 77), in illumination we can also speak of the beast initial as an imaginative variant of the figure initial (fig. 78). However, it is not in southern France but in Burgundy, at Cîteaux, the founding house of the Cistercian Order, that the demonic initial was given the most radical treatment. Here interlace in all its varieties is joined to the metamorphosis of form, to conjure up before us the shapes of initials in a pyrotechnic display of pictorial wit. Where shortage of space for these interlaced creatures presents a problem, the narrowness of the body of the letter is no handicap for the illuminator but provides a welcome excuse to strive for maximum density of entwinement. One creature treads on another's head, winds himself around his opponent, butts him, bores through him, and is himself seized and overcome by an adjacent demonic hybrid. Each figure is at once conqueror and conquered.

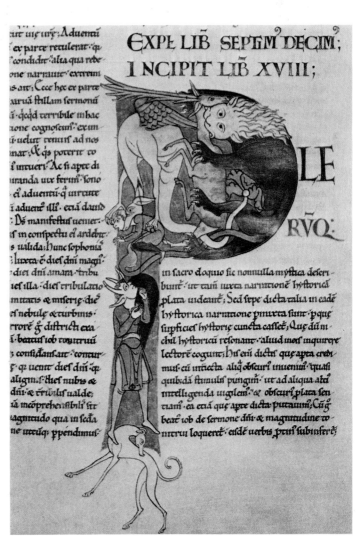

78
Initial.
Gregory, Moralia in Job.
Cîteaux, early 12th century

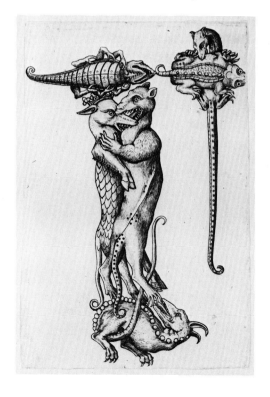

The imaginative Romanesque figure initial soon disappeared from the page, but it enjoyed a brilliant sequel in the late Gothic. This time, however, it was on the periphery of the illuminated book. In the fourteenth century, French miniaturists revived the fantastic figure initial but without unleashing a chaotic war of demonic creatures, and more importantly, not so much in the decoration of books as in that of documents (fig. 79). Just as archaic pen-flourishes were used in documents until quite recently, there was an attempt even then to elevate the appearance of the text by the inclusion of old-fashioned initials. The next logical step was a complete figure alphabet in a pattern-book, that of the Milanese artist Giovannino de' Grassi (pl. xxx). In the mid fifteenth century, this was taken by a German engraver, Master E. S., as a model for a series of engravings (figs. 80, 81), thereby producing works which were valued in their own right and independent of the milieu of the book to which they owed their origin. The shape of the initial had become an artistic goal in itself, its function as a vehicle for reading was at an end.

In our brief survey of the history of Sacramentary and Missal decoration (Chapter I), we were able to follow the evolution of the Te Igitur from a merely emphasized first letter, a simple initial (fig. 38), to a massive interlaced letter (fig. 39), and further to the Canon miniature (fig. 48); and we saw the change of the Preface initials VD from a simple abbreviation mark to a magnificent ornament which in its turn became a point of departure for figural-pictorial work.

This development could easily be misinterpreted – as if the growth of a simple ligature into a monumental monogram, capable of filling or dominating a whole page, was the direct outcome of Sacramentary decoration. It was not. The development of Sacramentary decoration depended rather on the fact that the ligatured initial became a major focus of artistic endeavour; this occurred in the seventh and eighth centuries within an Insular Irish–Anglo-Saxon setting. In that context it was, above all, part of a radical change of concept about the relationship of script and decoration, without which the independent development of the medieval beast initial would not have been possible.

When the initial, that accentuated first letter of script, came into being – already in the classical book (fig. 51) – its utilitarian function, as a marker, was predominant. As already pointed out, the unbroken line of classical script resisted penetration and the addition of any kind of eye-orienting aids; it tolerated the different paragraph signs more or less as one would an interloper and tended to eliminate them from the line of script and push them into the margin (fig. 50), a convention which naturally helped the design of the script on the page. This separation was also more in keeping with the aesthetic viewpoint of Antiquity which abhorred the mixing of spheres of expression. Each medium had its own set of self-circumscribed rules; there was thus an aversion to the mingling of elements such as script, decoration and picture. The earliest examples of initials which are more than enlarged letters are found thrust out into the margin. Furthermore, the initial is clearly separated from ordinary script by its essentially larger format – as if the two belonged to two different categories.

On this point, even in the oldest Irish manuscripts, as in the so-called Cathach (Psalter) of St. Columba (fig. 82), dated c.600, a wholly different attitude can be observed. Irish scribes tend to provide a gradual transition from the initial to normal-sized script, and further to draw the initial in from the margin to the column of script – not to treat it as a foreign element. The beginning of the line of the major

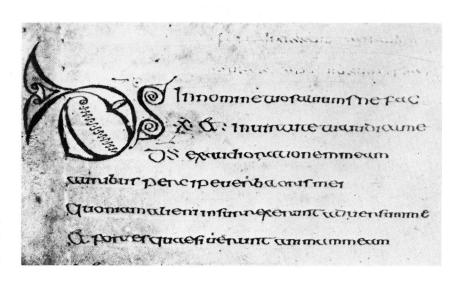

82
Initials.
Cathach (Psalter)
of St. Columba.
Insular, c. 600

83
Incipit
to St. Mark's Gospel.
Book of Durrow.
Insular, c. 680

text divisions gradually decreases to the size of the ordinary script in a kind of diminuendo, from the height of the initial or monogrammatic ligatures, from its dotted contours emphasized by the use of red ink, from its flourishes and similar ornamentation down to the pedestrian, simple letters of the script written in ordinary ink. At this level and in this kind of script, it is evident that calligrapher and illuminator were as a rule the same person.

From these modest beginnings three-quarters of a century later, c.680, at the time when the first surviving Irish, or rather Hiberno-

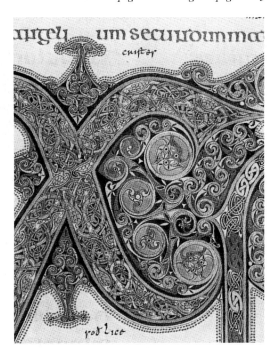

85
Chi Rho (detail).
Lindisfarne Gospels.
Insular, before 698 (?)

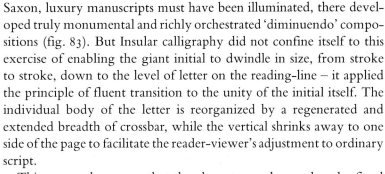

Saxon, luxury manuscripts must have been illuminated, there developed truly monumental and richly orchestrated 'diminuendo' compositions (fig. 83). But Insular calligraphy did not confine itself to this exercise of enabling the giant initial to dwindle in size, from stroke to stroke, down to the level of letter on the reading-line – it applied the principle of fluent transition to the unity of the initial itself. The individual body of the letter is reorganized by a regenerated and extended breadth of crossbar, while the vertical shrinks away to one side of the page to facilitate the reader-viewer's adjustment to ordinary script.

This means, however, that the character no longer has the fixed traditional shape predetermined for it in the Roman alphabet, and that it can change according to special circumstance, something that would never occur in a classical letter. The Insular initial, on the contrary, reveals itself as an elastic organism full of dynamic energy with the capacity to extend or shorten the parts of its body at will and thus, in observable measure, to alter its whole appearance; this often makes it difficult to recognize.

Curvilinear ornament – of old Celtic ancestry, going back to the La Tène style (fig. 84) – which fills the structure of the initial or adapts itself to it (fig. 85), contributes a blurring of forms and an impression of flux. The spirals in which the stem of the letter may end suggest by their rolling and unrolling a reversible movement. Consequently, the eye is caught in a labyrinth and distracted from firmly aligned reading. The smothering of letters in ornamentation – which recalls the tattooing of the body in primitive peoples – and thus the remorseless obscuring of legibility, the conflict inherent between the rational function of the letter and the value placed on

84
Ornamental metalwork.
Celtic,
early first century A.D.

87
Carpet page (detail).
Book of Durrow.
Insular, c. 680

the initial as a symbol of magic, all this testifies to a unique historical phenomenon. It is evidence of a collision and inter-penetration of two very different and ancient cultures, the barbarian and the Mediterranean, and the triumph or at least the revitalization of a prehistoric style imposed on a Christian cultural object, the Gospel Book, a classical legacy to Christianity.

We must bear in mind yet another aspect of this phenomenon: the Renaissance of Celtic and Teutonic zoomorphic ornament also brought with it an ornamental vocabulary indigenous to and developed in metal work, the art of the goldsmith (fig. 86), which now invaded the domain of book decoration (fig. 87). Although the Insular artist was practising his handiwork in the service of the Church and in a different medium, he obviously had not changed his aesthetic canon, his artistic sensibilities. The page of the book, the empty unwritten leaf, was for him an opportunity to give free rein to his urge to ornament all available space, leaving nothing empty; in other words, the page exercised the same stimulus on the calligrapher and illuminator as did the metallic surface, whether of weapon, jewel, or chalice, upon the Insular goldsmith. We know that the illuminator's decorative fantasy took control of the whole page of the book, decked it out with a profusion of ornament, and placed it as a consummately non-objective, not even symbolic, frontispiece at the beginning of the Gospels, the Preface to the Mass, the Canon and the like (pl. IV).

86
Gold buckle
from Sutton Hoo.
Celtic, mid 7th century

88
Chi Rho.
Book of Durrow.
Insular, c. 680

But the pagan impulse to shape the initial through elaboration and convolution had a more lasting and decisive effect on the future of illumination.

In pre-Carolingian Continental illumination (and contemporary with the Insular art just described), the initial also became a major artistic stimulus (figs. 60-62); but only in Insular art did it conquer the whole page of the book (fig. 54). This conquest took place in the Gospel Book which at that time, probably as a missionary's tool, was the most important among liturgical books. There were not four but five places in the Gospels which could most suitably provide an excuse for artistic embellishment: not only the beginning of each Gospel, but also the short section at the beginning of the book of Matthew, which tells the story of the Nativity after giving Christ's genealogy. At this point, the scribe-illuminator soars to new heights and sets in pride of place, in enormous dimensions, the ligature of ligatures, the Christ monogram, the Greek *XP* (Chi Rho), cushioned by smaller, ever-diminishing characters (pl. III). In one of the oldest Insular Gospel Books, the *XP* (fig. 88) is still inserted in the middle of the text; gradually it came to dominate the whole page (figs. 89, 90), in a

89
Chi Rho.
Gospels.
Insular, c. 750-760

relatively short span of time — from the end of the seventh to the
eighth century. The monogram page is always rather like a fortissimo
chord dying down in a gradual diminuendo. Legibility is certainly
not an aim of the scribe-illuminator (it is not infrequently reduced to
a minimum): he wished above all to give visual expression to the
excitement evoked by the mystical sound of the Nomina Sacra.
Words behave thaumaturgically, as if they were living figures in
pictures. The holy monogram is not intended to be deciphered, to
be read; like the sign of the cross, it is meant to be apprehended
spontaneously. And similarly, the script shapes grow into structures
developed from the ligatures of letters of the 'Liber generationis'
(fig. 91), 'Initium ...' (fig. 93), 'Quoniam' (fig. 54) or 'In principio'
(fig. 92), which possess the richness and pathos of pictorial compositions. As magical sign, the word replaces the picture, becomes itself

90
Chi Rho.
Book of Kells.
Insular, after 800

91
Opening to
St. Matthew's Gospel.
Lindisfarne Gospels.
Insular, before 698 (?)

a 'picture'. And thus in late products of Insular illumination the monogram or initial swells to the size of the page, spilling, as it were, the following line of script overboard; it becomes the sole content of the page.

The monogram or initial page proved to be a permanent gain for western illumination; without this invention on the part of Insular art those momentous developments of Sacramentary decoration – the Preface and Canon signs and symbols – would not have been possible. The textual reform of the Sacramentary inaugurated by Charlemagne had only provided the liturgical preconditions. Carolingian art took over the Insular device (fig. 93, cf. fig. 83) but not without creatively altering it. The Court School of Charlemagne, the atelier that produced manuscripts formerly known as the Ada group, had accomplished a reform of script aiming at classical clarity; but the magic of

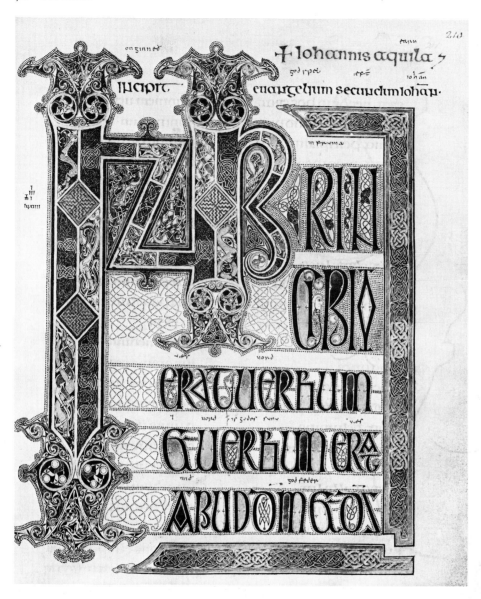

92
Opening to
St. John's Gospel.
Lindisfarne Gospels.
Insular, before 698 (?)

the large Insular Incipit and monogram page was not excluded, and the almost classical canon of the book was often enlivened by the application of pagan Insular ornament. To the magic of Insular origin was added another: the decorum of gold script (Chrysography) and purple parchment (pl. IX). Both these new elements were borrowed from imperial power-symbolism and were intended to convey the aura of this power in showing the omnipotence of God's mercy. In their frontispieces, the Carolingians certainly did not go to the extreme of a complete disintegration of script into purely ornamental compositions, but they did continue the earlier incantation of reader and observer through a monumental and magical combination of characters arranged in a sliding scale of graded lines of script. The ornamentation of script now lies in the gilding and not in the flourishing of the letter. This is a dignified display script, schooled in the

93
Opening to
St. Mark's Gospel.
Gospels of Saint-Martin-des-Champs.
Court School of Charlemagne,
late 8th century

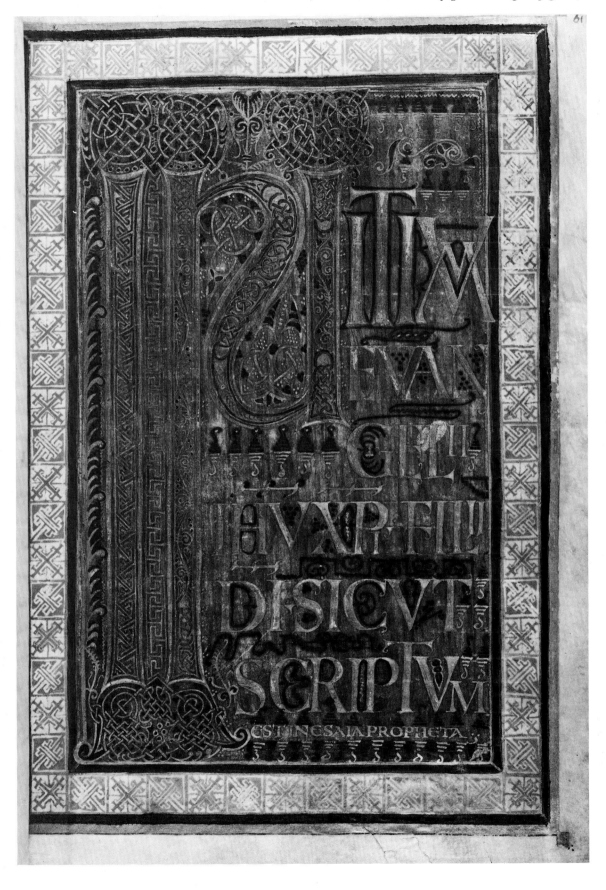

majuscules of classical epigrams and dedicated to giving the book the character of a timeless inscribed monument. Rows of single, short, classical lines, one above the other, (pl. VIII) balance the vertical impact of the powerful initial on the opposite page. The final consolidation of the vertical axis of the page is then completed by the formation of a rectangular border (where, alongside meander and other classical ornament, we also find Insular interlace) which holds the script and the gigantic initial compressed and bracketed. The script-area itself is framed like a figural scene, a pictorial composition. The frame separates the inner core of the page as display space from the untouched empty margins.

In two late-Carolingian schools, one northern French, the so-called Franco-Saxon, and the other that of St. Gall, the Insular idea of an outsized initial-composition was particularly popular, indeed underwent a kind of Renaissance. Both were located in regions with old

94
Beatus initial.
Psalter of Louis the German.
St. Omer, second quarter of 9th century

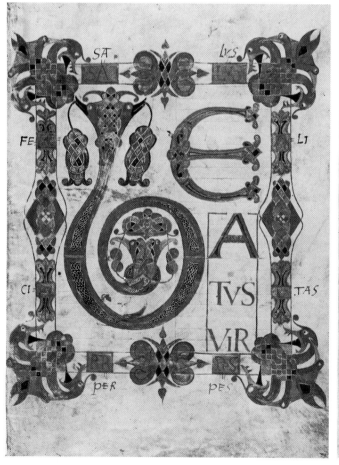

95
Beatus initial.
Salaberga Psalter.
Insular, second quarter of 8th century

96
Opening to
St. John's Gospel.
Gospels from St. Vaast.
Franco-Saxon, mid 9th century

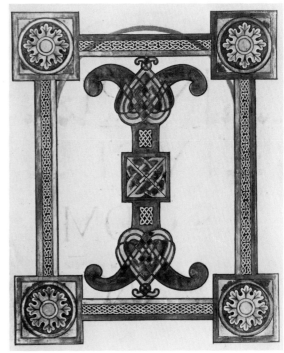

97
Initial.
Gospels.
Franco-Saxon, 9th century

Insular monastic foundations, and consequently Insular cultural tradition had never been wholly effaced by the Imperial Renaissance. We need only look at a Franco-Saxon Beatus Vir initial (fig. 94) beside one from one of the few remaining Insular Psalters (fig. 95) to see the unmistakeable relationship. As opposed to the Beatus initial executed by the Court School, the two are very closely connected, as much by the shape of the letters as by their ornamental vocabulary, particularly in the characteristic knots and spirals. The broken E of the Insular EA ligature was to enjoy special favour in the Franco-Saxon Preface sign (fig. 40). In Franco-Saxon illumination, the affinity with Insular art is so deep that the figural element plays a very subordinate role (fig. 96) and the book is decorated predominantly with ornament, and in fact with abstract ornament. Here, the concept of the splendid Incipit page was developed even further in a most original manner. Both schools bear the characteristic stamp of Carolingian art in that the initial-compositions are enclosed in architectural frames as they are in the books of the Court School (fig. 97). However, like the mature products of Insular art, the initial or initial-ligature has here absolute priority over ordinary script and is sole master of the page. It sees itself as the very centre, as the *raison-d'être* for the frame, and indeed is also sited in the actual geometrical centre of the page.

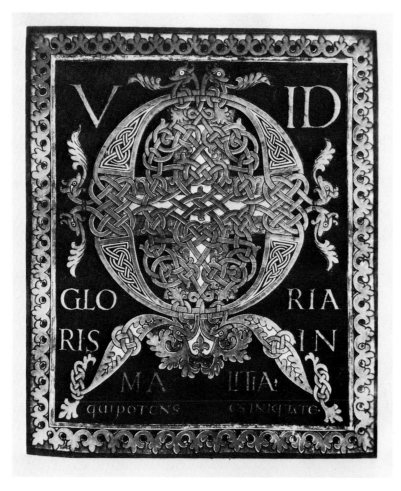

98
Initial to Psalm 51.
Folchard Psalter.
St. Gall, third quarter of 9th century

This entails a radical reorganization of the page. The decorative scheme has first priority in this style, even if it disturbs the sequence of letters determined by language. Thus it can happen that the initial, in contrast to its original location, is not the first letter that appears on the page with the rest of the lines of script following. In the 'Quid gloriaris' of the Folchard Psalter we find that the letters that come after the Q are pushed out above it (fig. 98), because the rounded tail of this particular character appeared to the artist to invite a certain symmetry of composition, and to this end he deliberately misplaced the first letter out of sequence. However, the St. Gall artist did not rest content with that: he went further and changed even the shape of the letter itself. In accordance with its new, centralized, position, the Q doubles its tail and also unfurls small termini horizontally as well as vertically along the axis of the tail, completing the symmetrical arrangement of initial page and indeed suggesting the shape of a cross spread over the surface of the letter. One single emphatic initial now occupies the whole width of the framed page, leaving little room for the remaining letters which must be accommodated in whatever space is still unoccupied. Fragmented into small groups of letters, the script

99
Initial to Psalm 41.
Egbert Psalter.
Reichenau, late 10th century

shelters on either side of the giant initial like a troupe of small footmen assembled around a powerful feudal lord. The leap from normal display script and display capitals to the initial is in this case so enormous that the question of a gradual transition from one format to the other seems here to be no longer valid.

The compositions created at St. Gall in the ninth century formed the foundation for subsequent tenth-century developments in the School of Reichenau, an island monastery on Lake Constance, north of St. Gall. It is in this school that the Ottonian style, if not first forged, then certainly came to fruition. Here was achieved an absolutely unequalled mastery in the invention and ornamental arrangement of the Incipit page, to rival any pictorial composition in status and monumentality. Rebelling against the restraints of the frame, these initials have a vitality never before witnessed. Their dynamism is apparent in every interlace and knot, forming and reforming, overflowing the boundaries of the core of the letter, sending out tendrils in all directions until they hold the ridge of the frame in their grasp (fig. 99). The framework becomes a prop rather than a boundary or superimposed enclosure. And finally, quite subtle and refined painting

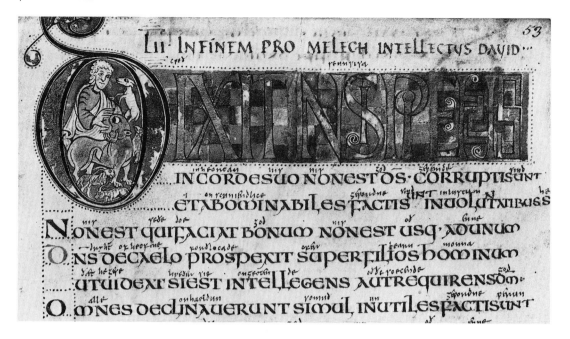

100
Initial to Psalm 52.
Vespasian Psalter.
Insular, c. 735

techniques help to emphasize the awesome magnitude of the symbol of Holy Script. Initials and frame are edged in purple (pl. XIV), and submerged in this purple band are occasional foliage and chimerae, as in a deep stream (pl. XV). The eye sees forms dimly, as if through twilight. Out of this night of purple and sharply contrasted with it, the ivory colour of the parchment inside the frame materializes. The initial, shining forth in gold, thus rises from a ground which seems twice as light by contrast. Thus, with the help of a night-like purple (not the only ground colour, as would be the case in classical 'Purpur' manuscripts), a three-tiered colour hierarchy is established: the brightness of daylight breaks through from inside a night-dark border, but these two opposite extremes are merely foils for the gold initial whose radiance eclipses and whose light transcends all. These Ottonian initial compositions, conceived in a fantasy of abstract colour, take us a long way from the monogram pages of Insular codices like the Book of Durrow (fig. 83) or of Lindisfarne (pl. III). In the Ottonian initial, no single ornamental motif is comparable: every vestige of linear construction has been obliterated, all articulation of pattern translated into colour values, vocabulary and syntax radically revised; and yet the Ottonian initial 'pictures' are only the last metamorphoses of ideas about form which were first broached in Insular art three hundred years earlier.

In elevating the initial to the position of picture-substitute, to a structure equivalent to the picture, we have by no means exhausted the list of artistic achievement which medieval initial-composition was able to stimulate. We must also look at the type of initial in which the letter does not represent a figure, in which it is not even constructed from it, but rather provides an arena *for* it. It does so in

101
David rescues the lamb
from the jaws of the lion.
Silver plate.
Cyprus, 613–630

102
Beatus initial.
Winchester Bible.
Winchester, c. 1150–1180

Sed in lege dni uolumtat ei· & in lege eius medita
bitur die ac nocte·   *Tamquam suo·*

two different ways: either the body of the letter serves as frame for a pictorial filling (fig. 127) or as support, display area and living space for a figural representation (fig. 124). We call the former an historiated, the latter an inhabited initial.

To the first category belong properly only initials with apertures, with internal space, as it were, which can contain or shelter figures or indeed whole scenes. A special case in the historiated initial is presented by the circular O treated like a pictorial shield, the medallion filled with a frontal face or a bust. The comparison between an O and the frame of a shield was too obvious to have been overlooked, even in schools where the historiated initial was not favoured. The earliest occurrence of an historiated initial is to be found in Insular art of the early eighth century and, in fact, in a Psalter which comes from Canterbury.

In the oval of a Q there is a scene from the life of David as a young man (fig. 100), a scene with iconography of eastern, early Byzantine origin (fig. 101). The Insular illuminator transplanted and embedded a narrative scene of independent existence as a picture into the special framework of a page of script and used it to close the aperture of an initial. Whether he had a forerunner in this is not known; but this significant innovation, with such great potential, could not have happened much earlier for various reasons. At any rate, the first historiated initial known to us shows all the signs of a beginner's struggle in mastering a new problem.

In the Byzantine model, David was represented as a shepherd, tearing open the jaws of the lion to free a lamb of his flock. In translating this scene into an historiated initial, the ground underfoot has been removed from the centre of the composition, and thus one sees several lambkins, using the outline of the figure of David like a path, as it were, climbing steeply upwards into space. The world of figures has found a new area of existence in which established laws of naturalistic or illusionistic pictorial space no longer suffice. Some hundred years later, the theme was taken up again by a byzantinizing artist, one of the illuminators of the Winchester Bible, who came closer to the early original composition (fig. 102): David leaps upon the back of the lion, wrenching open its jaws which have half closed around the lamb. A problem has been posed which was to occupy the medieval illuminator continuously from now on – the problem of reconciling the requirements of pictorial space with that of the painted surface of the page of the book.

At first the historiated initial appears not to have made much headway; we only find it again in Carolingian art and even there not very early, and only in one of the great schools, at Metz, under Bishop Drogo, in the second quarter of the ninth century. The Metz Master, extremely original in all his work, had acquired a rich treasury of imagery predominantly from eastern Early Christian art; and this he incorporated into a style of book decoration that consisted almost exclusively of ornamented initials. From antique art he took not only the greater part of his figurative vocabulary (cf. figs. 103, 104) but

103

105

104
The Three Marys at the Tomb
and the Ascension of Christ.
Ivory. Northern Italy, c. 400

also the ornamental forms – his primary decorative motif is the acanthus. It is not, however, used as a filling of the field, of the shaft of letters or of the border, as in classical art, but it climbs like a creeper or ivy along the body of the letters, enfolding and clasping them, or sprouting forth at the ends. The botanical element is a living plant which overgrows the dead and rigid scaffolding of the letter – an extremely fruitful idea that would one day celebrate a great triumph in Anglo-Saxon and Romanesque art. It is also worth noting that in the major work of the Metz Master, the Drogo Sacramentary, vine and foliage are not green, as one would expect, but gold with red outlines (pl. XII).

Now these entwined initials accommodate, for the most part and wherever possible, narrative scenes. And this happens not only where the arch of a letter makes a natural picture frame, as in the O: even the letters of the Preface and Canon in the Sacramentary are extremely individual designs. In both, pictorial content has a direct reference to the action of the Divine Service, the celebration of Mass. In the Preface (fig. 105), an enormous V is imposed upon the text all of which is written in majuscules in the classical manner. The upper end of the shaft of the V supports small architectural structures of which one, depicted as a church with a spire, encloses a half-figure of a priest celebrating Mass before the altar, and the other shows the sacrificial Lamb worshipped under the aedicule of the heavenly temple. The architectural designs rest like head-stops on the initial. In the Te Igitur

106

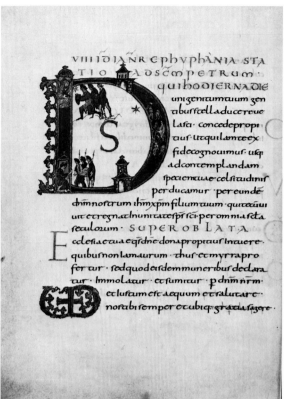

107

103, 105-107
Historiated initial C
with the Ascension of Christ;
Preface initial; opening of the Canon of the Mass;
historiated initial D with the Adoration of the Magi.
Drogo Sacramentary.
Metz, between 850 and 855

(fig. 106), the scenes were inserted into the specially-shaped openings in the stem and crossbar of the T. The Old Testament prefigurations of the Crucifixion (The Sacrifice of Melchisedec, Abel and Abraham) have here found accommodation as decoration of the crossbar. This represents a new freedom in layout for which the initial of the prayer at the Feast of the Nativity (pl. XII) is one of the most beautiful examples. The single episodes of the Birth of Christ, that is, the essential components – the lying-in of Mary, the crib with ox and ass, the bathing of the Child, the shepherds – these nest in different positions on a monumental C which is embedded in the middle of a broad column of script. One of these scenes, the group of shepherds, found no place in the interior of the letter – vines branching off from the end of the letter form a sling which balances them – they are found outside the stable, in the landscape. In another example, the form of the initial structurally contributes to the narrative. The D of the Epiphany initial (fig. 107) presents the story of the Magi in a sequence of three scenes: the first, the Magi before Herod; the second, their journey to Bethlehem; and the third, the Adoration of the Child. The first and third scenes are placed one above the other, but the looping curve of the D becomes the path which leads the second scene from one locality to the other in the course of the narrative. The structure of the initial, determined by its identity as script, becomes a stage for the action.

108
Putti harvesting grapes.
Porphyry sarcophagus.
Early Christian, c. 350

For a long time, very little notice was taken of this new concept in the relationship of script, picture and ornament as found in the initials of the Drogo Master. In the Carolingian as well as in the Ottonian period, a clear division between narrative and decorative aspects was as a rule preferred, and thus books were decorated on the one hand with pages of pictures or on the other with purely decorative initials (pls. XVI, XVII). The great moment of the historiated as well as of the inhabited initial came only when illumination recognized the significance of a wholly distinct concept of form which had developed in a quite different medium. It was the *motif of the inhabited scroll*. The illuminator had first to make its acquaintance, and only then could the different types of inhabited and even the historiated initial be fully developed.

The inhabited scroll had already been used in classical relief sculpture as a kind of playful motif. There are numerous decorative reliefs of the Roman period with scroll-work enlivened by animals, birds, even putti and small figures. We know of some reliefs whose foliage in its involutions forms a kind of row of medallions with small scenes, for example, the grape harvest (fig. 108). In Early Christian times the

109
Grape-harvest. Sarcophagus
with the Good Shepherd.
Early Christian, 4th century

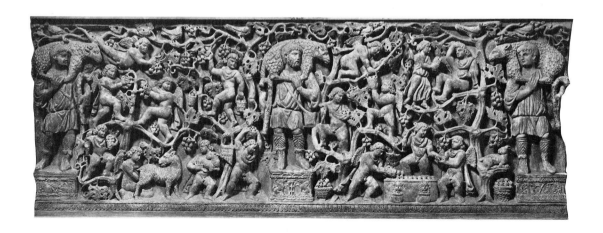

110
Scroll-work with hunting scenes.
Ivory. Northern France (?),
9th-10th century

111
Fragment of Irish
stone cross from Easby.
Northumbria, late 8th century

symbolism of the grapevine gave rise to compositions in which a grape-vine trellis spread out in endless undulations and sheltered in its branches pastoral scenes such as that of the Good Shepherd grazing his flock (fig. 109). Decisive for future development of the motif was a change first found in Insular stone-carving and in Carolingian ivories (figs. 110, 111) perhaps with forerunners in antique art. The idea first raised here is that there is a certain antagonism between plants and animals or between plants and men, a conflict which manifests itself in the plant tendrils acting aggressively towards the moving, living creature and restraining its freedom of movement. The bodies and limbs of animal or man are caught in the scroll as in a snare of creepers, and they offer resistance. In the knotting together of the two, antagonistic forces are held in check and the law of gravity seems suspended. A life-like, not inorganic, material is created from the interlace thus formed and this holds firm in every place and at every height.

Still in the first half of the tenth century, we suddenly find Anglo-Saxon initials appropriating these particular types of motifs that had apparently been found only in relief sculpture earlier on (for example in fig. 112, a bird caught in a D-initial grabs hold of a sprig with its beak). Curiously, in the flowering of Anglo-Saxon illumination that followed, hardly any attention was paid to such motifs; it did appear,

112
Initial.
Junius Psalter.
Winchester, second quarter of 10th century

113
Initial to Psalm 109.
Psalter. Saint-Germain-des-Prés,
mid 11th century

however, in northern and western French schools which were strongly influenced by England, schools like that of St. Bertin around 1000 or those later at Arras and Paris (St. Germain-des-Prés, fig. 113), and above all, in the flourishing Norman school with its numerous monastic centres. Common to all these schools of the eleventh century is the fact that the full-page picture remains an exception, frequently confined only to a title-page – in striking contrast to the fondness for pictures in Anglo-Saxon and also Ottonian art – and the decoration of the book concentrates on the ornamental initial. In Norman painting particularly, one can see a clear tendency not to allow figural elements free play but to immure them in ornament whenever possible (fig. 114). This gives the appearance of regarding the free-standing picture as something suspect and trying to hide it in a thicket of ornamental artifice, that is, in the structure of the initial. It would seem that the pictorial cycle of the Anglo-Saxons was usurped from its proper domain; and what the Normans took from it in the form of narrative art was transferred in diminutive form to the microcosm of the initial, and through the initial, subordinated to the page of script. Figures born free now become scroll inhabitants. Degrading the pictorial scene, however, means an ennobling of the initial – its elevation from being a peripheral subject, standing between the zone of anonymous ornament and anthropoid imagery, to that of a central position in representational art (fig. 115). Narrative has migrated to the space of an initial.

In the eleventh century, in the early phases of this process, we still see for the most part the anonymously inhabited scrolls in conflict with their environment. To the struggle of animal or man with surrounding plants which confine them, bind them or entangle them, is added the struggle of man against animal or demon, animal-man hybrids, often in double or treble entanglement (fig. 116). Or the curling scrolls can form a stage for a hunting scene in which hunter,

115
Initial.
Ambrose, Gospel Commentary.
Norman, 11th century

116
Initial. St. Augustine,
Commentary on the Psalms.
Rochester, c. 1100

114
Initial.
Bede, Gospel Commentary.
Norman, 11th century

as well as prey, is lost in the maze of the thicket of foliage. The creatures vie with one another and with us, concealed in that unbounded and yet claustrophobic continuum, the never-ending undulations of the scroll-work of northern medieval art.

In a Gospel Book executed around the year 1000 in the monastery of St. Bertin on the Channel coast in northern France, scroll-work of this type appears, as far as we know, for the first time (fig. 117). Instead of filling the border of an Incipit page flatly with acanthus leaves, as was usual in many Carolingian schools, and indeed as is the rule in this particular manuscript, the artist here placed a running acanthus scroll in the available margins, and this provides the framework for housing figures and animals. In the spaces hollowed out

117
Border frieze with hunting scenes.
Gospels. St. Bertin, c. 1000

118
Capital with bear hunt.
From the Cloisters of the
Augustinian Monastery in Toulouse.
Southern France, late 12th century

within the winding scroll a kind of tubular shaft is formed and small
scenes of the hunt unfold. Some time later quite similar subjects
will be found in northern French illumination, even in initials[29] –
gymnastically inhabited scrolls.

It is worth mentioning here that this rediscovery of a motif found
earlier though only sporadically in pre-Carolingian and Carolingian
art now gave manuscript illumination the lead in a process of development in which monumental art followed some distance behind. The
inhabited scroll became a favourite decorative subject of Romanesque
sculpture, that is the new monumental art, although not until about
a century later. A twin-capital from the Cloisters of the Augustinian
monastery at Toulouse, forms a frieze showing a bear-hunt which
transposes and translates the inhabited scroll of illuminated manuscripts into carved stone (fig. 118). In sculpted objects, especially in
ivory carvings on book covers, there are many parallels, and many
motifs are found both in illumination and in sculpture (fig. 119).

Yet it is not always anonymous play that takes place in the shadows
of the encircling scroll, as if in hiding. In the illuminated books of
north-western France and those influenced by them, there are often

119
Ivory corzier with Nativity.
English, 12th century

Beatus initial.
Psalter. St. Gall, 9th century

single biblical scenes or a series of scenes integrated into scrolls. The genesis of the Romanesque fusion of figure and ornament can best be followed in the development of the large Beatus initial at the beginning of the Psalter. This was the initial *par excellence* and it stimulated the ornamentalizing impulse of the medieval artist to ever-increasing heights of fantasy.

The first of our examples is an initial from the mid ninth century which, it should be emphasized, originated in an environment dominated by the ideals of a great past, the pre-Carolingian Insular epoch: it is the giant Beatus initial of a Psalter from the school of St. Gall, painted in silver and gold (fig. 120). The first impression is one of impenetrable interlacement of forms, and yet the principle of construction is very simple. The shaft of the letter is anchored on the page and in the script by a ribbon-interlace which terminates at opposite ends above and below in birds' heads, while the ends finish

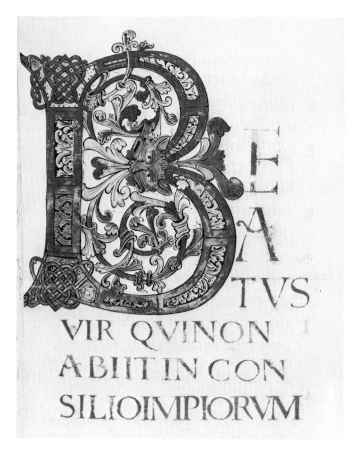

121
Beatus initial.
Harley Psalter.
Winchester, c. 980

off in intersecting foliate bands in the middle. It is not a very massive
shaft, and it would be slimmer still were it not for the (oxydized)
silver filling of the opening that encloses the gold interlace. The birds'
head terminals, turned right, break the bows of the B which spread
laterally outwards, crossing and interlacing in the middle. In this
double-arch, not entirely symmetrical, we are once again in the sphere
of the kaleidoscopic initial; the bands are changed into the hind-
quarters, torso or heads of animals which resemble birds and whose
backsides end in tails; these, in turn, finish in scrolls with berries upon
which small birds feed. The ends of the scrolls, however, curve under
and above these birds. The outward curve of the lower, larger bow
of the B is surprisingly insubstantial and is filled with scroll-work.
Nowhere is there a pause or stasis; everywhere there is kinetic self-
change and endless intertwinement. We have no significant Beatus
initial from Insular art of the eighth century, but the St. Gall example
will serve as an adequate substitute.

If the St. Gall Beatus B can serve to illustrate a missing Insular
version, then the majestic Beatus B of an Anglo-Saxon Psalter of the
tenth century may also represent an initial still conceived in the spirit
of Carolingian classicism (fig. 121). Although executed in England,
specific Insular elements are quite firmly suppressed. The ribbon-
interlace is limited to the two horizontal hinges of the initial. The

zoomorphic element is still visible in the beaked terminals of the interlace and in an imposing lion's or cat's mask from whose jaws pour forth a thick proliferation of acanthus scrolls as from a gargoyle. Even the botanic element is found in the form of an acanthus frieze which fills the compartment of the initial but is greatly reduced in the vertical shaft and bows of the body of the B. The body of the letter in this example provides a clear, solid framework for the initial with emphatic consolidation in the joints. The dynamism of plant life is contained. The shaft and bows of the initial, filled with a plant frieze, enclose and confine the scroll-spirals which unfold in the interior of the letter.

When, a century later (in 1060, shortly before the Norman Conquest), an English Psalter was given an imposing Beatus B (fig. 122), the structure of the initial remained virtually the same, but a new element was added to its vocabulary of forms – the figural. Figures

122
Beatus initial.
Arundel Psalter.
Winchester, c. 1060

tatg·
elita
ı
tın
bo
ı epat
·quɾ·
naɣ.
ıhu..
ım.
ıdeſ
ueſ
·
ugıu
efu.
·ahı
ſ
ſtra.
utt.
umı.
ua
heɾ.
eſpe·
ıte·
ıcıpıɿ

QVI NON ABIIT IN CONSILIO IMPIOR·
& ınuıa peccatoɿ. ñ ſtetıt. et ın cathe·
dra derıſoɿ non Sedıt.
Sed ın lege· dñi uoluntaſ eſ. & ın lege eſ

123
Beatus initial.
Carilef Bible.
Norman, late 11th century

are interpolated in the spirals of the scroll. In the upper bow of the
initial, a young man in Phrygian cap tries to pick his way through a
thicket of scroll-work, his legs entangled in the stems of the plants;
below, King David balances on a seat precariously formed from the
spiralling stems. Both are examples of inhabited scrolls. But the
inhabited scroll-initial is found earlier in Normandy and also in Paris,
and so we see here that Norman influence affected art in Britain even
before the Norman Conquest. One cannot exclude the possibility that
the miniaturist responsible for this Psalter from Winchester trained in
Normandy, and a Norman schooling can certainly be assumed for
the illuminator who decorated a great Bible for the first Norman
Bishop of Durham, William of Carilef. Even he follows an early
Anglo-Saxon format (fig. 123), except that he eliminates the central
lion's mask as a device for joining the two bows of the B by the
simple expedient of interlacing them. In so doing, he enables the
spiralling scrolls to begin at the ends of the shaft of the letter and not
at a lion's jaws, and from there to emerge from a beast's jaws.
From this beginning, the scrolls curl themselves into spiralling circles
forming the bows of the letter. Here, in the upper compartment, a
quadruped and not a human figure struggles against the encumbering

124
Beatus initial.
St. Augustine, Commentary on the Psalms.
Norman, late 11th century

plants. The lower circling scroll holds David 'enthroned' with harp – surely an author-portrait which has found refuge in the initial.

There are, however, even Norman Beatus initials in which the initial structure houses entire narrative sequences. On the Incipit page of two Norman commentaries on the psalms, we find a complete David cycle submerged in the labyrinth of a large B-initial (fig. 124).[30] After some searching, it is possible to identify individual episodes, single elements garnered from different initials: David rescuing the lamb from the lion's jaws; David and Goliath; David with his psaltery; and perhaps even reduced fragments of other scenes. The novelty of this is that the initial, in this example, has become a stage of action; from being affiliated primarily to the text and events described in it, the initial (and this is characteristic of Romanesque art) has progressed to become the theatre for figural art *per se;* and

INCIPIT TRACTAT⁹
PSALMORVM
AVGVSTINI EPI :

125
Incipit.
St. Augustine, Commentary on the Psalms.
Norman, second half of 11th century

the laws of naturalistic or illusionistic pictorial space no longer apply: in other words, a space continuum has been shattered. Figures now have a two-fold problem – dealing with adversaries (attack or defence), and finding secure footing in the twisting vine, as if all movement can only take place within this scaffolding of entwinement. As in Romanesque sculpture, every figure is bound to the articulated parts of a structural mass as the defining space, so in the same way, its existence is here bound to the space provided by the body of the letter and its physical limits.

In order to view the phenomenon of a co-existence of figure and ornament within a letter in the right perspective, we must remember that those scriptoria and centres of illumination in which the assimilation of figures into the script was carried through most efficiently did not, as a rule, care much for independent or free-standing pictures with figures. The figural picture, if used, appears only as a portrait of the author or a title-page composition (fig. 125), not as narrative illustration. But even this kind of subordination of figure representation to its surrounding script did not last long: by the first half of the twelfth century, a movement had begun in all European art centres (France, England, Germany, Italy, Spain) which was to make representational art more independent, also within the framework of the book.

126
Incipit to the Acts of the Apostles,
Ascension of Christ.
Giant Bible. Central Italy,
first half of 12th century

This movement towards autonomy of figurative art revolutionized
both Psalter and Bible illustration. At the same time it tended to make
miniature painting dependent on large-scale painting. In countries
like Italy, where the illuminated book had never been a matter of first
priority, a monumental style was, to all outward appearances, more
or less transferred to illumination (fig. 126). But elsewhere, in France
and England for example, where illumination indisputably ranked
high among the fine arts, the dialogue with representational forms
developed in other media generated new forms and styles that genu-
inely belonged to the illuminated book. It is to this last development
that we shall now turn.

In the late eleventh and early twelfth centuries, France seems to have been the leading country in the sphere of illumination; but around 1120 the centre of gravity shifted to England. About this time a Psalter was executed in the monastery of St. Albans, a place named after the protomartyr of England and of no artistic significance until then. In this Psalter there is a powerful movement towards representational art and pictorial narrative. In the Beatus B (fig. 127), the initial's interior has suddenly been emptied of all ornament, which is now confined to filling only the initial's framework. In its construction, ribbon-interlace at the corners, animal heads at the start of the double-bows, nothing has changed. But the interior of the double-bows is treated like a single pictorial area: the figure of David with harp overlaps the division between upper and lower compartments of the letter, so that the author of the psalms can give ear to the inspiration of the dove (more like a swan) of the Holy Ghost descending from above. And instead of a precarious seat on a tendril − compare the Norman parallel some thirty years earlier (fig. 123) − the Psalmist is established securely on a solid throne. Fundamentally, the initial now has two levels − a picture has been projected upon an initial. This is no longer an inhabited initial; it is historiated. We must go back several centuries, back to the artists of the Corbie Psalter, to find a similar kind of filling for an initial (fig. 128).

All the psalm initials in the St. Albans Psalter are historiated (fig. 129). In addition, between the Calendar and Psalter proper, a

127
Beatus initial.
St. Albans Psalter.
St. Albans, c. 1119–1123

128
Beatus initial.
Corbie Psalter.
Corbie, c. 800

129
Initial.
St. Albans Psalter.
St. Albans, c. 1119-1123

130
Entry into Jerusalem.
St. Albans Psalter.
St. Albans, c. 1119-1123

separate sequence of pictures from the Life of Christ has been inserted – a narrative cycle in full-page pictures without any text (fig. 130). The book thus represents a sudden dynamic impulse towards pictorial expression, which is meant to act upon us just as surely as do text and decorative elements developed from the script.[31] It can be inferred from a long commentary on the Beatus initial, probably written by the artist himself, and from notes of an apology on another folio which defend pictorial representation in the Church (an extract from Gregory the Great's famous letter),[32] that unqualified support for the picture *qua* picture must have seemed something new and perhaps risky. In short, in the St. Albans Psalter we have a kind of counter-movement against the iconoclastic tendencies of Norman and Romanesque art. This resistance, which gained its strength through its growing receptivity to Mediterranean and contemporary Byzantine art, won a victory over the abstract art of ornament derived from script. The process can be followed most clearly in the history of Bible illustration, which suddenly becomes very relevant. Before turning to that subject, however, there is still one after-effect of the history of the inhabited initial which must be mentioned.

Again we return to the Beatus initial. After the St. Albans Psalter this initial was still primarily a decorative structure, also in most luxury manuscripts; but there was no longer an interweaving of scene and ornament. The double-bow of the B now rather becomes the frame for two pictures, as in the Ingeborg Psalter (fig. 131) which

was illuminated in Tournai c.1200; occasionally, as in the example cited, the lateral curves of the B are extended to create medallion-shapes which are filled with scenes from the life of David. But there was a retrospective trend, particularly in English manuscripts, motivated by a desire to rescue the ornamental character of the traditional Beatus initial by introducing an iconographic theme in which botanical entwinement was representationally justified: the *Tree of Jesse*. This picture of the genealogy of Christ from the beginning of St. Matthew was certainly not invented for the Psalter. Iconographically, it dates from the early Romanesque period (fig. 132). The metaphor of a genealogical tree, however, could best be understood as a type of inhabited plant. Thus, around 1200, the Tree of Jesse was first implanted in the Beatus B, there to weather the transition from being an inhabited initial (fig. 133) to being celebrated in baroque proliferation right up to the fourteenth century for the veritable orgies of its winding form (pl. XXVII).

131
Beatus initial.
Ingeborg Psalter.
Tournai, early 13th century

132
Tree of Jesse.
Lambeth Bible.
Canterbury, c. 1145

133
Beatus initial as Tree of Jesse.
Huntingfield Psalter.
English, late 12th century

Colour plates

*The measurements listed
refer to the dimensions
of the original folio.*

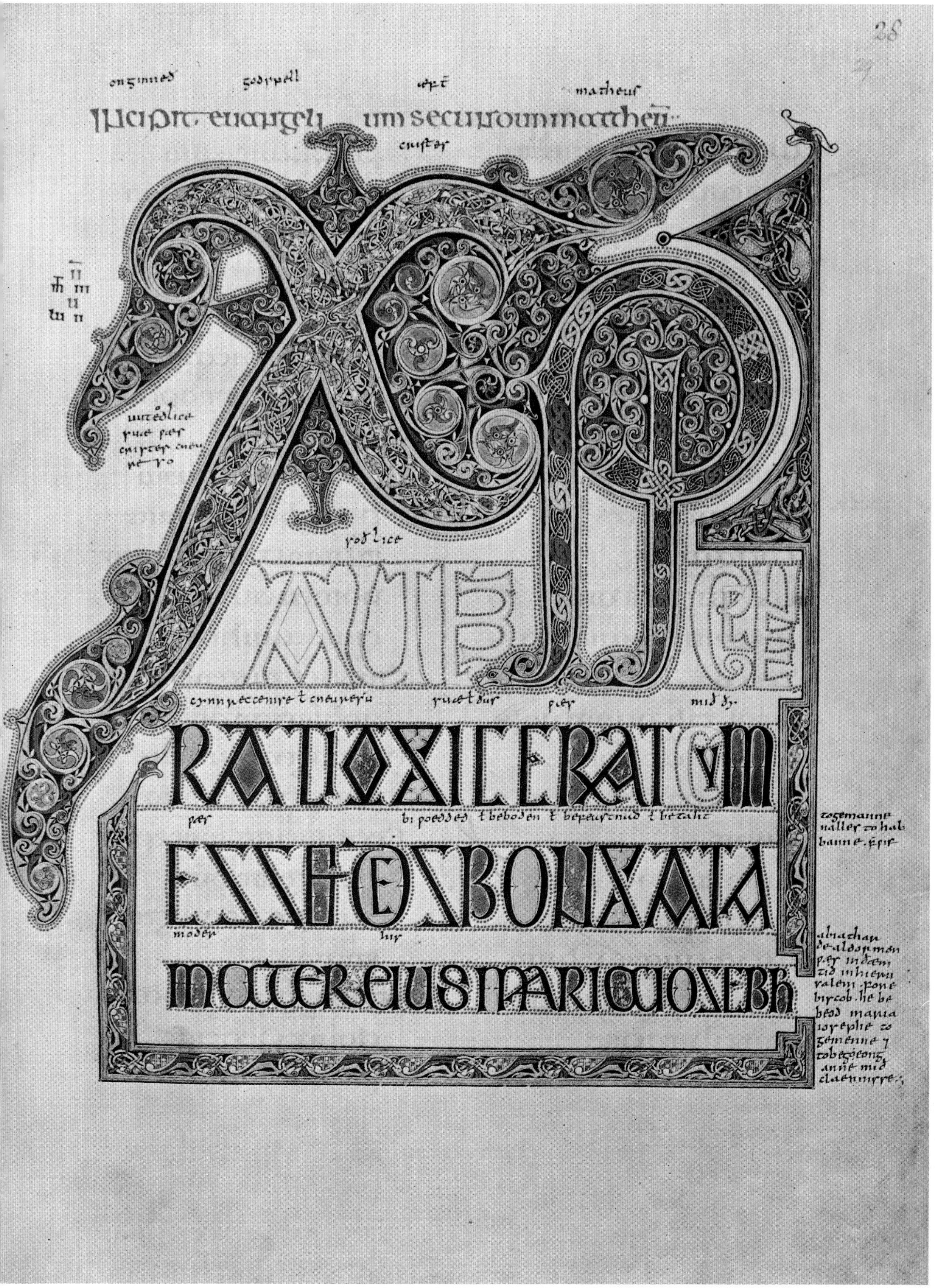

IV

f. falur aircham f cimulch. iudru f. iudnerch. Dedencif f. Nobif: epi copuf. teli
ngud racerdor teiliau. dubnuno. ecculielin filiu epi. Sarnbiu cum ibien. et fulzen
neif q hi fidele recuppit...q cuftodiennt li decnetf. libcatuf bleidiud z plif fit
q hi ncuftodiennt. Sit maledict; a do ec acuiliau incf euanngelio fcnipf; et
ur plf fue fiat...

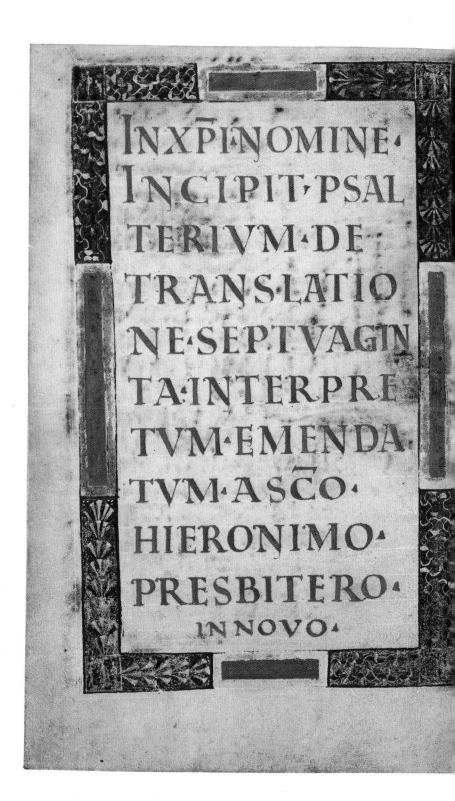

IN XPI NOMINE
INCIPIT PSAL
TERIVM DE
TRANSLATIO
NE SEPTVAGIN
TA INTERPRE
TVM EMENDA
TVM A SCO
HIERONIMO
PRESBITERO
IN NOVO

BEATVS VIR· QVI NON ABIIT IN CONSILIO IMPIORVM ET IN VIA PECCATORV NON STETIT· ET IN CATHEDRA PESTILEN TIAE NON SEDIT·

X

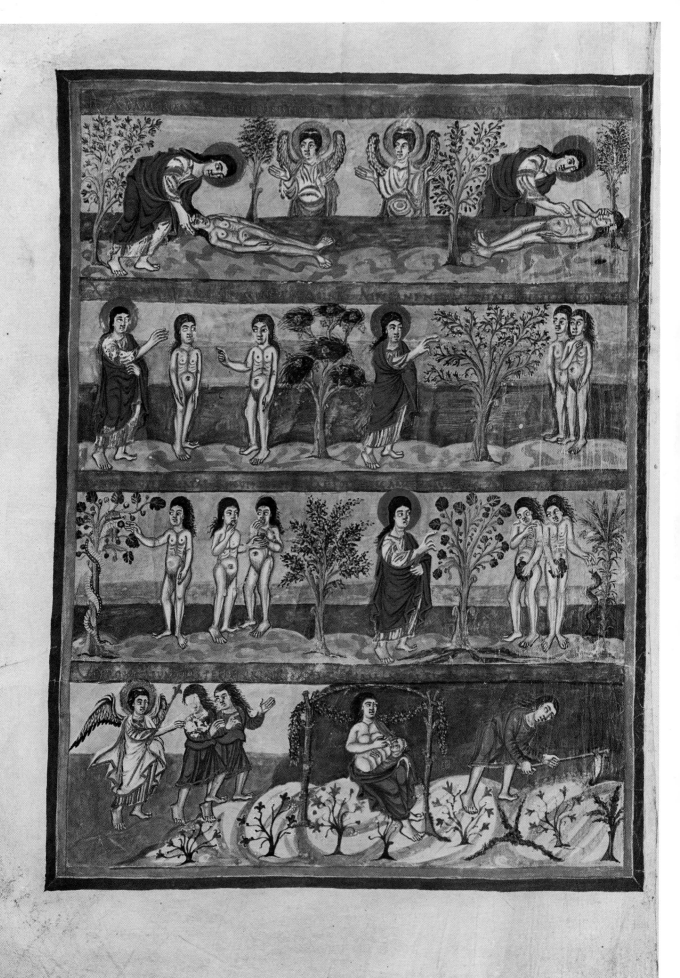

IN NATONIA DS̄CM PETRUM
ONCEDE C̄S OMNIPOTENS DS̄ UT
NOSUNIGENITI
TUINOUA
PER   CARNEM
NA   TIUITAS
LI   BERETQUOS
              SUBPEC
              CATIIUGO
              UETUSTA
              SERUITUS   TENET
              PEREUN   DEM
              DN̄M NOS   TRUM
              IHM XPM   FILIŪ
              TUUM QUI
              TECUM
UIUIT   ETREG
NAT DS̄
INUNITATE
SP̄SSC̄I · PER OMNIA SC̄LA SC̄LO RUM ·

BER
GENERA
TI
I

XVI

IN FINEM PRO
SALVVM MEFAC
dñe qm defecit scs
quo diminute sunt ueri
tates afiliis hominum ;
Vana locuti sunt unusquis
que adproximum suum
labio doloso. incorde &
corde locuti sunt mala ;
Dissperdat dñs uniuersa
labia dolosa. &linguam
mali loquam
Quidixerunt linguam ñram

OCTAVA   PSALMVS
magnificabimus. labia
ñra anobis sunt. quis ñr
est dñs
Propter miseriam inopum
& gemitum pauperum ·
nunc exurgam dicit dñs ;
Ponam super salutare
meum. fiducialiter aga
ineo
Eloquia dñi eloquia casta ·
argentum igne examina
tum. terre. purgatum

DAVID · XI ·
septuplum
Tu dñe seruabis nos. & custo
dies nos. ageneratione hac
ineternum
Incir cuitu impii
ambulant. scdm altitudi
nem tuam multiplicasti
filios hominum

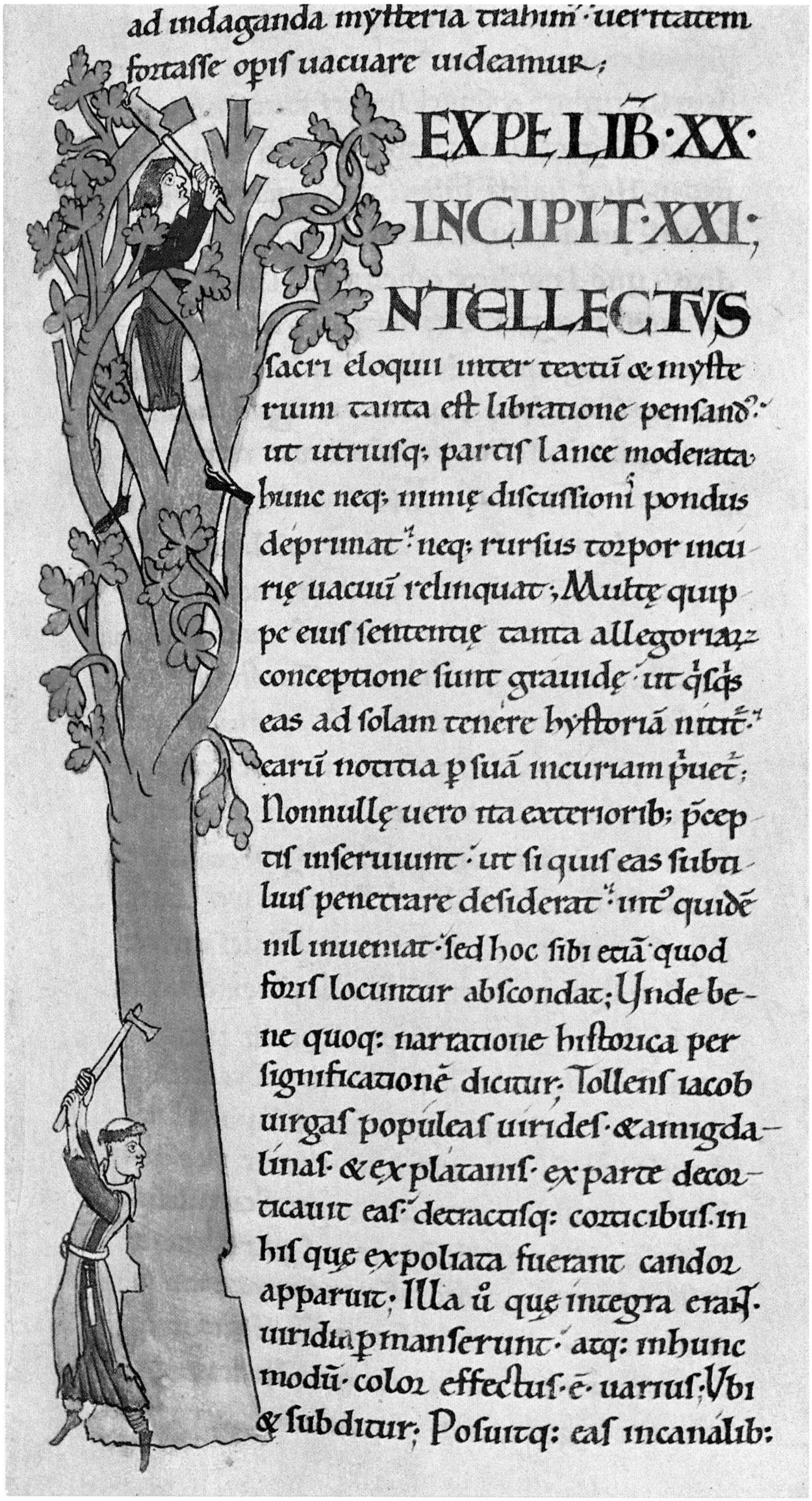

ad indaganda mysteria trahim̅· ueritatem
fortasse opis uacuare uideamur;

EXPĿ·LIB·XX·

INCIPIT·XXI;

NTELLECTVS
sacri eloquii inter textū & myste
riū tanta est libratione pensand̅·
ut utriusq; partis lance moderata
hunc neq; nimię discussioni pondus
deprimat̅· neq; rursus torpor incu
rię uacuū relinquat;·Multę quip
pe eius sententię tanta allegoriarᷓ
conceptione sunt grauidę· ut q̅s̅q̅s̅
eas ad solam tenere hystoriā nitit̅·
earū notitia p suā incuriam p̅uet̅;
Nonnullę uero ita exterioribᵬ· p̅cep
tis inseruiunt· ut si quis eas subti
lius penetrare desiderat̅· int̅ quidē
nil inueniat· sed hoc sibi etiā quod
foris locuntur abscondat; Unde be
ne quoq; narratione hystorica per
significatione dicitur; Tollens iacob
uirgas populeas uirides· & amigda
linas· & ex platanis· ex parte deco
ticauit eas· detractisq; corticibus·in
his quę expoliata fuerant candor
apparuit· Illa ū quę integra eras̅·
uiridiap̅ manserunt· atq; inhunc
modū· color effectus̅ ē· uarius; Ubi
& subditur; Posuitq; eas incanalibᵬ:

INCIPIT LIBER ELLES MOTH. QVI GRELEDI CITUR EXODUS:

qui ingressi sunt inegyptum cu iacob: singuli cu do
mib; suis introierunt. Ruben· symeon· leui· iuda·
isachar· zabulon & beniamin· dan· & nept alim·
gad· & aser· Erant igit oms anime eoru qui egressi
sunt defemore iacob· septuaginta quinq̃: Ioseph

tuisum est aliud signum
in celo. Et ecce draco mag
nus et rufus habens capita sep
tem et cornua decem. et in capiti
bus suis septem diademata. Et
cauda eius trahebat tertiam par
tem stellarum celi et misit eas in
terram et draco stetit ante mulie
rem que erat paritura. ut cum pe
perisset filium eius deuoraret. Et
peperit filium masculinum qui rec
turus erat omnes gentes in uir
ga ferrea. Et raptus est filius ei
ad deum i ad thronum eius et
mulier fugit in solitudine ii ha

ler locum paratum. a deo ubi paf
cant illam dieb; mille ducentis
sexaginta. Draco iste diabolum signi
ficat. Rufus autem color ta
lis est ac si croceo colori sanguinem admisceas. i
Concordat uero pallidus color. i. croceus cum sa
guineo. quia sangus dum effunditur morte
adducit. palor autem totum corpus morientis
cepit. Recte ergo diabolus habere dicitur colore
mortis. qui illius inuidia mors intrauit in or
bem terrarum. Per septem uero capita reprobi qs
diabolus ad decipiendum genus humanum uisf
est designantur. Diademata eius potestatem desig
nant. Ipse enim est rex sicut dicit scriptura sup om
nes filios superbie. Nam sicut per septem cornua ag
ni omnes electi designantur quos in septem partes
diuisimus. ita et per septem capita draconis rep
bi qui eis in uia dei aduersari sunt designantur.
Primum namq; caput draconis fuerunt repro
bi qui ante diluuium fuerunt quos scriptura fi
lios hominum uocat. qui eis qui filii dei uocaban
tur in laqueum fuerunt. Per caudam uero q
finis est corporis antixpi designatur tertiam parte
stellarum celi cauda draconis traxisse uisa est. q
antixpe multos ex his qui ab hominib; electi pu
trahuntur. et qui in ecclia uelud stelle in celo scienci
a i intellectu refulgent decipere atq; i perditiois i e

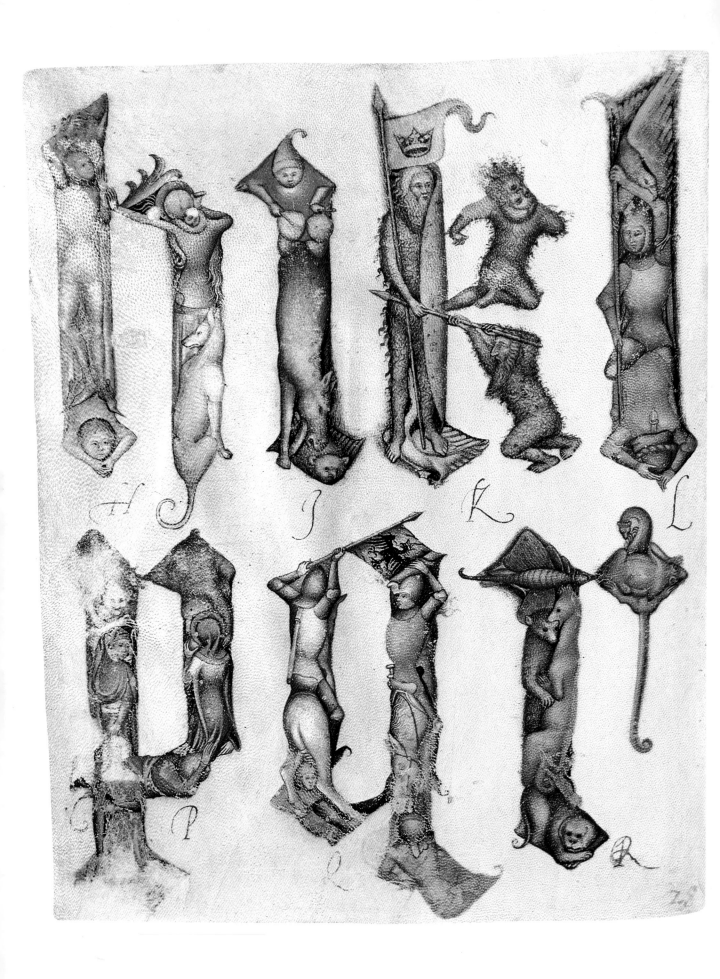

III · Bible Illustration

TWELFTH-CENTURY book illumination, as mentioned earlier, was particularly concerned with the decoration of the complete Bible, that is to say to give a continuous series of illustrations of the books of the Old and New Testament combined in a single work, often consisting of several volumes. Romanesque Giant Bibles form a class of their own among illuminated medieval manuscripts: their dimensions are 'out-size'[33] – the distinctive medieval *terminus technicus* for them was 'bibliotheca' – and it is the extraordinarily massive proportions that determine the format of these unwieldy folios. Although we now readily accept the idea of a collected edition of the Holy Scriptures in which each of the seventy different books is introduced by a kind of frontispiece, the concept of systematically illustrating the contents of the Bible was not formulated and carried into effect until the Romanesque period.

For more than a century efforts were made to achieve a fully illustrated monumental Bible, and all the great medieval nations took part in this artistic enterprise. In retrospect, it seems like an international contest of all the leading workshops, as if they had known of one another; where the original initiative came from – from France, England or Italy – is still not clear. In all centres, however, the early stages are characterized by experimentation and the search for appropriate solutions.

In Italy, the introduction of pictures into the Bible codex was effected wholly by appropriating forms from large-scale painting. In the early monumental Bibles, before and around 1100, there is rarely any attempt to integrate the individual figures that stand at the beginning of books as author-portraits into the surrounding text or initial. They are positioned free-standing on the bare ground of the page (fig. 134) and, to anchor them there, they are at best flanked and enclosed by majuscules. Later, as richer narrative illustration became more abundant, scenes precede the text in separate, thinly framed pictorial strips or full-page pictures. An inner contact between picture and script is never established, and the picture remains a cumbersome alien body in the book. It plays no part in formatting the page, nor does it attempt to adapt its style to the specific requirements of its environment. In these early Italian Bibles, the choice of folio format actually facilitates the accommodation of images that come from larger-than-life sources. These illuminated books, which are among the largest of their type, are in effect miniature paintings in the sense of diminutives of wall-paintings (fig. 126).

On the other side of the Alps the situation is quite different, even in such schools as Salzburg where dependence on Italy was very strong. In the earliest Bible from the Salzburg circle, that from the monastic library of St. Florian (fig. 135) – upon which, to start with, Italian hands had collaborated – some historiated initials begin to appear among those in the more usual Italianate-geometrical style, and these are the first signs of a reawakened desire for pictorial expression. In the design of such initials, we find a perfect analogy with the contemporary Beatus initial of the St. Albans Psalter (fig. 127); the figural or scenic elements either project awkwardly into the aperture of the letter or are stuck on to it. The first fully illustrated Salzburg Bibles, those from Michaelbeuren[34] and Admont (fig. 137), already distinguish sharply between ornamental initials and framed pictures, which are set apart from the text and often full-page. At this level, the affinity to the Italian Giant Bibles is at its greatest, but the Salzburg volumes give additional emphasis to the geometry of the book-page in the arrangement of picture, initial and script; the modulation of heterogeneous elements is more harmonious and the effect more

134
Tobias as Prophet.
Opening to the Book of Tobit.
Giant Bible from Hirsau.
Rome or Central Italy,
second half of 11th century

135
Joshua is commanded by God
to cross the Jordan.
Opening to the Book of Joshua.
Giant Bible from St. Florian.
Northern Italian, c. 1075

136
Scenes from the life of David.
Gumpert Bible.
Bavaria or Salzburg, before 1195

planned. In the most mature creation of Salzburg Bible production –
the Gumpert Bible at Erlangen, pictorially the richest of all Salzburg
Bibles – picture and script are indeed still separate, but now the
pictorial page is given a decorative scheme that is compatible with
the established demands of surface-ornamentation. Single scenes have
become pictorial inlays in an ornamental patterning (fig. 136). So we
see that, in the North, the book-page did manage to achieve some
decorative order. And we shall gain a better understanding of the
means by which Salzburg painting achieved this order when we look
at the question of the relationship between picture and frame, rather
than that of picture and initial.

Siquis acceperit uxorem & uixerit in ei rem cur
pem; cxviiii
Siquis acceperit uxore in racem. non exiet ad bellu cxx
Non pignorabis mola cxx
Si captus fuerit fur cxxi
Quare habe que fecerit dns marie cxxii
Debitore u fenerabis puim cxxiii
Inpignore pauperis non dormies & mercede labo
rantis ne tarde reddideris cxxv
Non mortem patres p filiis cxxvi
Non declinabis indiciu aduene & orfani & uidue
Non pignorabis uidua cxxvii
Si secaueris segete cxxviii
Si liges oliuam cxxviiii
Si uindemiabis uinea cxxx
Si iudicaueris impuii dabis ei xl flagellos cxxxi
Non infrenabis boue triturante cxxxii
Si quis mortuus fuerit quis habens uxore sine fi
liis accipiet ca fuit ei cxxx iiii
So noluerit homo accipere uxore fris sui cxxxv
Si rixauerint duo homines inse cxxxvi
Non erit tibi pondus iniquu & mensura dupplice
Inme habe quanta tibi cxxxviii
fecerit amalech cxxxviiii
Cu intrueris tterra qua dns ds dabit uobis
Et dixit moyses cxl
ad ppl'm tacere & audire cxli
Hi stabit benedicere plebe & hi maledicere
Maledict' omnis cxlii
qui fecerit hec cxliii
Si custodieris p cepta dni uenient super uos be
nedictiones omis cxliiii
Si non audieritis uenient uniuos maledictiones
iste; cxlv
Uocauit moyses oms filios isrl' & dixit ad eos scitis
quanta fecerit dns pharaoni p pt' uos cxlvi
Quare sit absconsa do que aut pala nobis
Prope est uerbu inore tuo cxlvii
& incorde tuo cxlviii
Ecce dedi ante oculos tuos uita & morte cl
Et consumauit moyses omia uerba ista cli
Et uocauit moyses ihesum & dixit ei uiriliter age
& conualesce clii
Dixit dns ad moysen tu dormies cu patrib; tuis &
fornicabitur plebs hec post deos alienos
Scripsit moyses canticu hoc cliii
Dixit dns ad moysen ascende inmonte abarim &
morere ibi clv
Benedixit moyses homo di filios isrl' clvi
Mortuus est moyses intra moab clvii
Et non fuit p pha misit sicut fuit moyses

EXPLICIUNT CAPITULA

68

137
Moses receives the Commandments.
Opening to the fifth Book of Moses.
Giant Bible from Admont.
Salzburg, c. 1140

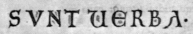

INCIPIT · LIBER
DEVTRONOMII

SVNT VERBA·
QVE·LOCVTUS·
EST MOYSES·
ADOMNEM ISRAHEL TRANSIOR
danen insolitudine campestri. contra
mare rubrum· inter pharan & thophel
& laban. & aseroth. ubi aurii plurimę
undecim dieb; dehoreb p uiā montis
seir usq; cadesbarne quadragesimo
anno· undecimo mense prima die men
sis. Locutus est moyses adfilios isrl
omnia que preceperat illi dns ut dicerẹ

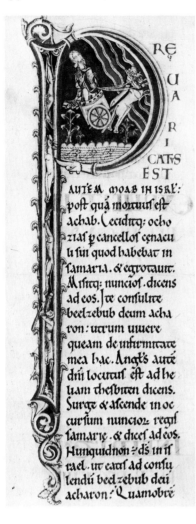

138
Ascent of Elijah.
Rochester Bible.
Rochester, c. 1130

139
Initial.
Medical Treatise.
Norman, c. 1100

Returning to Romanesque Bible decoration, however, we now look westward, from the eastern periphery of Europe, to the great English Bibles, which, as far as originality and quality is concerned, have few peers among contemporary illumination. In the beginning, historiated initials (fig. 138) are found in English as indeed in Salzburg Bibles; they continue to occur alternately with purely decorative initials but remain in the minority. However, it soon becomes clear that the inhabitants of English initials (that is, single figures as well as scenes) transcend their abode and venture further. For prototypes, they take the various gnomish creatures who populate a particular decorative type of initial in the earlier Norman style – initials known as 'gymnastic' (fig. 139) where the frame of the initial is used as jungle-gym for acrobatic exercises by the living – man, plants or animals. The letter becomes the stage for action: at the outset for merely decorative play, but in the end for solemn scenes from Holy Scripture.

In the English example of the Rochester Bible just cited, the Ascent of Elijah (fig. 138) is squeezed into the aperture of the curved head of an enormous P-initial, while the shaft of the letter is given over to the profane pastime of the hunt. The Elijah scene is an abbreviated

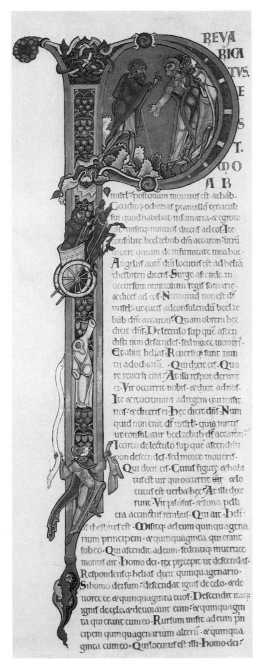

141
Ascent of Elijah.
Winchester Bible.
Winchester, c. 1150

140
Ascent of Elijah.
Dover Bible.
Canterbury, mid 12th century

version, since the complementary and essential figure of young Elisha (who has to assume the mantle of the translated master) is missing. In the Dover Bible (fig. 140), some twenty years later – and like the Rochester Bible a product of the Canterbury school – one can see this incomplete version of the legend, as it was found in the Rochester Bible, adequately completed. Here the shaft of the P is seen as an upward-moving path for the ascent to celestial heights. The curve of the P is the door to Heaven through which the chariot of Elijah will vanish from sight. Below, however, at the foot of the shaft of the initial, in fact on an offshoot of the vine, stands the young prophet awaiting the mantle of the master which falls towards him from above and with which he will work miracles. The corresponding miniature from the Winchester Bible (fig. 141), slightly later than the Dover Bible (that is, shortly after the middle of the twelfth century)

142
The calling of Jeremiah (detail).
Winchester Bible.
Winchester, c. 1180

offers a third version of the same subject. In it Elijah's chariot of fire
has moved to the shaft of the initial in order to make room for a
further episode above in the aperture of the P; Heaven, in this instance,
is located beneath the curve of the P. In an attempt to heighten the rich
visual effect of the Bible, the Winchester master has again obscured the
original concept of the composition.

From the hand of the master responsible for this initial, the first in
a succession of artists who worked on the illustration of this pictorial
compendium for half a century, there are initials which, superficially,
could be classified as inhabited (pl. XXIII), and others which could be
called historiated (like the P with the Ascent of Elijah). In the one,
the figures are placed among the vines, and in the other, there are no
vines. Basically, the type of composition is the same: but the Winchester artist no longer felt the necessity to ensnare his figures in a
mass of curling vines in order to accommodate them to the form and
essence of the body of the initial. The network which informs and
shapes his figures is no longer found outside but is invested in the
figures themselves. The threads from which the net is spun are the
pathlines of drapery (fig. 142). Just as the scrolls which form the
curvilinear basis of Romanesque art are, in the last analysis, of classical
origin, so paradoxically the internal net ensnaring Romanesque figures is developed from a classical concept of form. It represents, so
to speak, a travesty of the idea of the *dualism of clothing and body*. It is
well known that the Greeks discovered the secret of how to make

143
Victory
loosening her sandal.
Relief from the Temple of Athene.
Athens, Acropolis.
Attic, after 400 B.C.

145
St. Mark (detail).
New Testament.
Byzantine from Grottaferrata (?),
second half of 12th century

144
Dancing maiden (detail
from Isaiah in prayer).
Paris Psalter.
Constantinople,
mid 10th century

visible the living core beneath an obscuring and enclosing shell of dead material: in short, how technically to show clothing and yet sense the body (fig. 143). By creating the fiction of a diaphanous drapery, the way was made clear for presenting the figure clothed as in daily life, and yet allowing an occasional glimpse of the form of the body beneath the surface of drapery. At the same time, and this is the decisive point for our enquiry, the flexible material of the drapery, palpable in pull and pressure, is the medium by which the power agitating and controlling the body is effected and communicated to us. The essence of the matter is that the life of the human figure is revealed through an interplay of body and drapery; indeed, it only achieves form by this interaction. Byzantine art first inherited the classical tradition of diaphanous drapery directly, especially in the Macedonian Renaissance (fig. 144); but as a result of the dematerialization of all things corporeal, the drapery element notably won the upper hand in subsequent developments. The unity of folds and furrows in drapery created an enveloping linear and, for the most part, formalized system, which framed and grouped little islands or fragments of organic substance like quilting, breaking down the outward surface of figures into compartments. Something of the old tense truce between the two factors is still there, but one has the impression of a very attenuated, almost ungraspable, filigree spun around a translucent spiritual body (fig. 145). What we have before us is merely the symbolic formula of a conflict of forces.

English artists of the Romanesque period, especially those of the mid twelfth century, assiduously studied the Byzantine version of diaphanous drapery transmitted to them through various channels;[35] but they completely reinterpeted it with their particular Insular perspective and distilled from it a convincingly unclassical system of linear patterning. The ornamentally motivated Insular fantasy of form, a northern pagan inheritance, seized upon the idea of a network of folds, only latent in Byzantine drapery treatment, outlined it and reduced all modelling to small ribbons of shadows in the furrows (fig. 34). In the English translation of Byzantine models, the surface of the figure reminds one of an 'anatomical diagram' in which all the tendons, veins and arteries are outlined. The feel for the corporeal, which characterizes the tension between outer surface and inner core, has disappeared. The network of lines has become autonomous, something which manifests itself in a guise, not very physical, and able to change into self-willed, abstract movement bearing no relation to the objective requirements of movement in a figure. It is a characteristic of this style that single figures cannot be disengaged from a group. They are concealed, as it were, by the structure of folds and contours, so that they seem inextricable (fig. 146). In the ebb and flow of lines, organic form is dissolved; it becomes the plaything of an unleashed dynamism which seeks by the most incredible quicksilver changes to engage or elude our glance as in a labyrinth. In brief, in this kind of art the human figure has to defend itself against a self-generated and attacking force, just as earlier it had to assert itself against the vitality of encircling vine-scrolls. An enormous elasticity now distinguishes the human figure. Instead of depending on the help of undulating and interlacing scrolls, human figures are now capable of adapting themselves to the life-rhythm of the initials and to fill the entire space. By this means, however, inhabited initials are unexpectedly turned into historiated ones. The ornamentalizing figure has driven out ornament from the initial.

At this point of development, artistic currents made themselves felt which had come under strong Byzantine influence and were not willing to accept that figure and narrative composition should be subjugated to an extraneous systematization. It is quite revealing that in the execution of the Winchester Bible, those artists who were cosmopolitan and less insular found no satisfaction in initials and the space provided by initials. They wished to introduce proper, large and multi-compartmental pictorial pages in those major sections of the book which had not yet been illuminated. One of the artists employed learnt his pictorial narrative technique not in contemporary Mediterranean schools but rather from Early Christian art, which must have been accessible to him both in the original and in Carolingian translations. On one of the pages that he designed and that only exists as a drawing, the frontispiece to Maccabees (fig. 28), we can trace its ancestry from a forerunner in a Carolingian Maccabees manuscript from St. Gall (figs. 25, 26) back to the classical period; it is thus unrelated to contemporary Byzantine art to which his fellow illuminators were turning. An admittedly medieval element in his

146
Death of Saul.
Lambeth Bible.
Canterbury (?),
c. 1140–1150

ACTV̄E AVT̄E
poſtam moxtuuſ eſt ſaul uc

style was his attempt to reinterpret the painterly illusionism of his models by graphic means, that is in solid outline. It is perhaps not entirely accidental that we do not know how this gifted draughtsman painted. Everything he did was drawn only in outline, whether in the Winchester Bible or in the Terence manuscript at Oxford, itself a copy of a classical exemplar.[36] His work on the Bible, no less than that of his predecessor, remained unfinished.

Towards the end of the twelfth century, a team of artists, basically Byzantine-trained, joined the enterprise with the aim of providing colour for the unfinished outlines of the two older artists but, in many cases, all they did was spread a coat of modern colour over an existing drawing. There are, however, instances where this younger byzantinizing generation supplied both sketch and colouring.

Byzantine art, it will be remembered, was not familiar with the arrangement of figural elements within the initial – in the Middle Byzantine period there were indeed Byzantine figure initials, but no historiated initials. It is clear that for an English artist studying Byzantine style, the first priority was the necessity of integrating a Byzantine pictorial world, essentially monumental, into the latinate page of the book which was designed around the initial (fig. 147). Subjects at home in spacious pictorial fields had to be demoted, so to speak, to become the inhabitants of initials. Figures now found their own balance, their own weight, their own dignity, and their dynamics had to appear compatible with the rules of organic movement. There was no longer a question of a figure having to execute serpentine spirals or undulations with a view to nestling inside the curve of the bow of a letter or even of snaking upwards through or along its shaft. At first, there was still a tendency to fill the aperture of the initial with a span of figures; gradually, however, there was no hesitation in leaving the ground bare, especially since it was now no longer simply coloured, as in early Romanesque art, but covered with shining gold.

The triumph of the Byzantine aesthetic canon meant on the one hand an emancipation of figure composition from all ornamental formulas; on the other hand, however, this byzantinizing style could in compensation claim a special contribution to the decorative aspect of the book: in imitation of the gold ground of Byzantine mosaics, icons and miniatures, the ground of initials with pictures and those of free-standing illustrations were overlaid with gold-leaf. The history of the colour gold in the Middle Ages forms an important chapter which has yet to be written. It is not only the history of gold ground. In the early period, from Early Christian art up to the Carolingian and Ottonian period, indeed up to early German Romanesque, gold appears in the form of chrysography, under which term I group both gold script as well as gold interlacement and vine ornament executed in gold.[37] Chrysography in this two-fold application was, for example, popular in the Carolingian period (pls. VII, VIII, IX, XII).[38] At that time, at least in western Europe, a gold pigment of sandy, grainy character, with only a faint glitter, was used. It was not until the twelfth century that book-illuminators achieved the gold effect of the lead-enriched potash glass of Byzantine mosaics by the application of extremely thin, highly polished plate-metal gold, that is gold-leaf.

Because of its metallic substance, gold alone among the colours has a decidedly tangible material reality – a palpability – and, because of its costliness, an extraordinary value in decoration. It is thus *ipso facto* ornament, even when it is unpatterned. That gold as background covering could succeed in the late twelfth century in being universally accepted was largely the result of two factors: first, the technical innovation mentioned before, which brought the metallurgy of gold directly into use and, secondly, a spiritual attitude inextricably linked to this sensory phenomenon. Medieval gold ground was always interpreted as a symbol of transcendental light. In the light transmitted by the gold of Byzantine mosaics there was eternal cosmic space dissolved at its most palpable in the unreal, or even, in the supernatural; and yet our senses are directly touched by this light. In Sicily, Southern

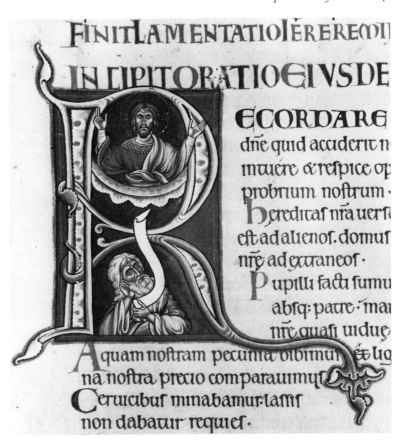

147
Initial with Christ Pantocrator
and the prophet Jeremiah.
Winchester Bible.
Winchester, late 12th century

Italy and Venice, and during the Crusades even in the Byzantine East itself, western painters and illuminators had learned about the use of dematerializing light. It was therefore a logical next step that they should strive to increase the sacral tone of their pictures by appropriating the celebratory gold light of Byzantine painting. The new gold-leaf made it possible to achieve the full gold brilliance at one time generally associated with the gold of Byzantine domes, apses and wall-decoration. From this point on, gold ground in the West remained *de rigeur* for sacral subject matter, even in late medieval panel-painting, and it was precisely there that it was eventually displaced in the temporal atmosphere of the new wave of realism.

The initials of the Winchester byzantinizing master show clearly that figure and ornament from now on will have to go their separate ways, that the common ground both elements had shared was disappearing. Since the human figure had, under Byzantine influence, gained an inner stability, it now loses its mercurial elasticity and sheds the hybrid quality of the anthropomorphic arabesque. It is now no longer capable of adjusting its form to ornamental requirements. On the other hand, plant ornament loses its ability to mimic the physiognomical, in short its animistic qualities, and becomes a purely decorative element. Ornament is now something solely peripheral and must content itself

INCIPIT
LIBER GE
NESIS:
N PRIN
CIPIO CRE
AVIT DEV
EV ET TERRÃ.

Terra autem erat inanif &
uacua · & tenebre erant
sup faciem abyssi · & sps
dei ferebatur sup aquas.
Dyxitq: df· Fiat lux · Et
facta est lux · Et uidit df
lucem quod ēē bona · &
diuisit df lucē atenebris.
Appellauitq: lucē diē: &
tenebras noctem · Factūq;
est uespe & mane · dies un̄
Dixit quoq; df· Fiat firma II.
mentum inmedio aquaru̅·
& diuidat aquas ab aqui.
Et fecit df firmamentum·
diuisitq; aquas qu̅e erã
subfirmamento · ab iif
qu̅e erant sup firmame̅ti·
Et factum est ita · Voca
uitq; df firmamentu̅ ce
lum̅· & factu̅ est uespe &
mane · dies secundus.
Dixit uero df· Congre III.

148
Genesis initial (detail).
Winchester Bible.
Winchester, c. 1150

with a secondary role, as an accessory or a filling – for example, as the space-filler for a rectangular frame that contains a sequence of medallions or mandorlas, as indeed became customary in Genesis initials among others, at that time. These are constructed of a series of medallions for the Six Days of Creation and all foliate ornament in pushed to the outside (fig. 148), where it sometimes bursts forth at the corners like some flamboyant pinnacle.

Once expelled from the initial, scroll ornament conquered new territory in the Gothic period. The ascenders and finials of letters are picked out along the margins of the text and embodied in scrolls or tendrils which curl up at the ends in a twist of circling spirals. The offshoots of vines serve as framing devices, their existence no longer originating internally from the script itself but clambering outside along the column of text.

In the early phases of development, these extensions of the initial completely fulfil their new geometrical role by framing the text; they deny their proper plant origin – except at terminals – and become straight border edging which here and there, like barbed wire, sprouts into spiky thorns (fig. 149). At this stage, one cannot even speak of

149
Illustration to Psalm 80.
Bird Psalter.
English, late 13th century

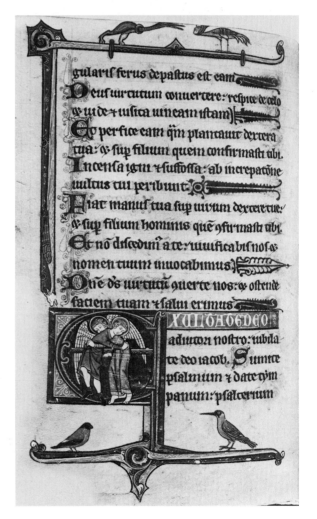

scrolls with thorny leaves; the borders have only thorns and no leaves. In the interim, however, French illumination had developed very delicately winding tendril borders, sprouting three- (or more) lobed leaves, and the commonly-used German term 'Dornblattranke' (thorn-leaf scroll work) suits this species, which surrounds the field of script in a gossamer enclosure (fig. 150). These climbing vines then in turn produce their particular fauna – Gothic drollery, a world of shapes that belong specifically to book-illumination just as, earlier, the inhabited initial had done, and to which the drollery is linked in numerous ways. Drollery offers not only the possibility of a free play of fantasy or humorous representation (fig. 23): in this border region, where censorship is not nearly as strong as in the illustration of Holy Scripture itself, we now see the start of a flow of genre motifs and other scenes from daily life, and it is here that the significance of the drollery and its future development lies (pls. XXVII, XXIX, fig. 151).

The sheer weightlessness of this type of book-decoration would not have been possible had not Gothic art subjected the format of the book itself to a radical transformation. In the late Romanesque, a powerful narrative and representational urge had tended to express itself in the detachment of illustration from script by allocating a separate pictorial page. Now an opposition sets in to counteract this excess of picture and ornament and to bring the book back to a more

150
Illustration to Psalm 68.
Hours and Psalter.
Paris, c. 1300

151
Text pages with drolleries.
Psalter. Ghent, c. 1320–1330

151a
Page from Aristotle, *Metaphysica*.
English, c. 1310

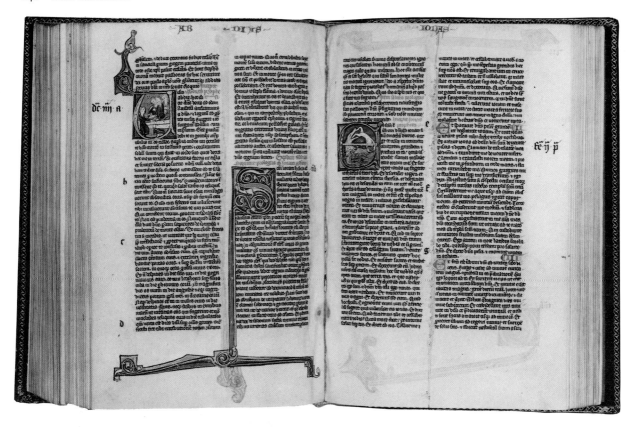

manageable format, abandoning the enormous size of both the book itself and the figures in it. Bible production and illustration now undergo a dramatic turning point: on the heels of Romanesque Giant Bibles now follow the smallest Bible manuscripts known in the history of this type; they are often less than 10cm high and contain the whole text of the Bible in a single volume. We know, however, what produced the sudden change: in the 1220's the University of Paris commissioned a new edition of the complete text of the Bible as a study aid in one volume and in a pocket-size format. To this end, script and illustration had to be microscopically small (fig. 152). These are proper miniature Bibles with appropriately minute and carefully concise ornamentation. The majority of these little Bibles are decorated, many with historiated initials in which a kind of pictorial shorthand is used to represent either the author of a particular book or a typical scene. Here, a genuine miniature style in the diminutive sense has been formed, curiously at the same time as the great monumental style of sculpture in cathedrals. The recognition that a form of painting had here emerged that was specific to the book and to no other medium must indeed be the meaning of Dante's famous description of 'that art which in Paris they call illumination'.[39] The moment the miniature Bible was born, the days of the monumental Bible were numbered. That must be the explanation of why so many of the great Bibles, like the Winchester Bible, were left with their decoration incomplete.

It can be said that the example of Byzantine painting had freed the figure from the embrace and ensnarement of plant ornament. Nevertheless, even here, its spatial existence has not yet become autonomous. Figures and scenes still have to submit to an outside order, this time to one borrowed from architecture. If we take a work of French High Gothic illumination, namely, the Gospels of Sainte-Chapelle from the latter part of the thirteenth century (fig. 153), we will see that the slender tall picture-columns which generally serve for I-initials are topped almost everywhere with baldachins in the form of Gothic roof-structures, gables, pinnacles, turrets and so forth. On closer examination, it is clear that these baldachins have no relevant significance, that they are not supposed to represent a particular structure mentioned in the narrative. On the contrary, the architec-

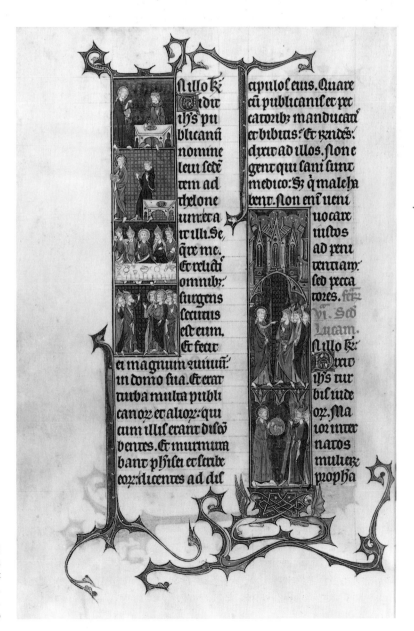

153
Christ with the tax collector;
John the Baptist
prophesies the Lamb of God.
Gospels of Sainte-Chapelle.
Paris, c. 1255–1260

154
Author-portrait.
Adam de la Halle,
Le Chansonnier d'Arras.
Northern France, late 13th century

155
John the Baptist.
Throne of Maximian (detail),
c. 520–550

tural superstructure appears regardless of whether the scene takes place inside or in the open. If architecture has to be represented for illustrative reasons, then the miniaturist has no hesitation in further covering the roof of the scenic background with an additional architectural pediment. The St. Louis Psalter, executed in France c. 1270, contains a lengthy series of full-page pictures inserted between the Calendar and the Psalter, as did many English or English-influenced Psalters of the Romanesque period. Each of these full-page pictures is framed by a border filled with trailing ivy; but, in addition, each scene has, on the inside of the frame, an architectural gable (pl. XXVI). Occasionally these superstructures form the border above, without being impeded by a decorative frame. They can then tower freely in the empty margin (fig. 154).

The origin of this motif is not difficult to guess. We are familiar with it from Gothic sculpture where every figure or scene has its own canopy, as if each separate being is obliged to stand in its own little sentry-box. In sculpture, the baldachin-top is a last reminder of the fact that the new three-dimensional figure had originally been hewn from a block, that is, out of a mass of stone, in which it was at one time embedded. Even after its emancipation as a Gothic column-

157
Canon Table.
Soissons Gospels.
Court School of Charlemagne,
early 9th century

156
Prophet from the
left portal of the west-front
of Chartres, 1145-1155

figure (fig. 156), it still holds fast to its original surroundings as if in its own shell. The motif of the canopy-crowned figure has a long history: it is another form of the 'arcade figure', the *homme-arcade* as the French call it, a compositional form first encountered in late Antiquity (fig. 155), where it was seen as a complementary pheno- menon to the disappearing free-standing statuary. The close link which the human figure formed at that time with its surrounding arcade remained in force in all its medieval derivatives both in sculp- ture and in painting. The superimposed arcade gave the human figure a base and stability which it was not able to develop on its own. And as a framed form, the figure could be incorporated into the page of the book.

The arcade figure first came to book illumination via the Roman- esque trumeau and the Gothic figure-column (fig. 156). Architectural forms and structures, however, had already been in use for a long time in illumination as a means of composing the page. I need only remind you of the arcading in the Canon Tables[40] of the Gospels (fig. 157) and the different types of arches under which the Evangelists and other author-portraits in frontispieces (figs. 35, 36) customarily appear.

In this context it is not inappropriate to comment briefly on the relationship between picture and frame in late-classical and medieval illumination. In classical times book illumination borrowed all forms of frame and ornament from the realm of monumental art – not only its motifs and ornamental vocabulary, but also the manner of their application. For the title of the book, the inscription would frequently be framed by a circular ribbon-like laurel wreath, the kind seen on gravestones or other monumental epigraphs enclosed in medallions (fig. 158). Instead of the inscription, Christian symbols could also function as front emblems to the manuscript.[41] Wherever we find such medallion-titles in medieval manuscripts (hardly ever later than in Carolingian books and in Byzantine art up to the tenth century), we have to infer a borrowing from classical models. After a hiatus of many years' duration, Italian humanists again produced this form of layout – a recreation perhaps without any classical example in mind, but simply prompted by deep affinity with a congenial tradition (fig. 159).

158
Title-page.
Vienna Dioscorides,
Herbal.
Byzantine, c. 512

159
Title-page.
Comedies of Terence.
Florence, 1466

160
Title-page.
Philocalus Calendar.
Copy of the Roman Calendar of 354

161
Title-page to St. Matthew's Gospel.
Gospels. Echternach (?),
late 8th century

Classical illumination had used yet another kind of title-page, but one which found little approval in the Middle Ages: the motif of a title-plaque held by two putti or genii, the *Tabula ansata,* as seen in the frontispiece of the Philocalus Calendar of 354, known to us from a drawing after the lost original (fig. 160). Here it is not the page itself that bears the inscription, but an object illustrated on the page. It is a specifically classical idea: not even the script is permitted to be flat, but must be, at least indirectly, translated into three-dimensional terms. In the Middle Ages, this idea, understandably, only found a sporadic echo. A relatively strong echo can still be found in a pre-Carolingian Gospel Book from Trier (fig. 161). Here the archangels Michael and Gabriel appear on the frontispiece to the Gospel of St. Matthew, holding a tablet with the Incipit to face the reader as observer. The tablet seems to be heavy, and therefore, in order not to tire the angels, a solid pillar is placed beneath it. Quite obviously this is a reproduction of a late-classical or early-Byzantine picture, and the paradox is that it was executed by an immigrant Insular artist for whom the familiar formula was a purely scripted Incipit. When our motif occurs in Ottonian art once again, the tablet of script which the angels hold is no longer a tangible object (fig. 162). The format of the tablet now reflects the format of the page; the angels present that page and the act of holding it has become merely a gesture.

162
Inscription for Christ in Majesty.
Codex Aureus of Echternach.
Echternach, before 1039

As in similar cases, early Renaissance humanism has in this instance
again rediscovered an old formula and recognized its significance:
script was not something to be set down on parchment, but was to
be perceived as the actual pictorial content of the page, something
which is primarily visual, not legible. In Padua, with its particular
interest in archaeology – among the circle of Squarcione, the first
owner and collector of plaster-casts of antique sculpture, and those of
his famous pupil Mantegna – title-pages were designed *all' antica* that
were worthy of any genuine antique codex. On one of these Paduan
title-pages (fig. 163), we find a marble base surmounted by two
magnificent candelabra; attached at the top is a parchment scroll,
which two putti are about to unroll. In another example, putti hold
a framed marble tablet on which there are two antique coins and a
large metallic capital initial, the continuation of the text to be read
on a roll below.[42] The most successful idea was that of an arch bearing
the inscription, either spanning an altar-shaped structure or suspended
from two putti above. The page of the book has changed itself into

pictorial space in which one looks upon an inscribed arch as upon a placard (fig. 164). In the engraved title-pages of Baroque books, there is a well-known sequel to these designs: in an idyllic landscape, putti in flight let a cloth bearing the book's title flutter in the air.[43] In the last metamorphosis of this motif, in a Piranesi frontispiece, there is a melancholy backward glance to a lost classical glory: in an expanse of rubble, we discover a broken boulder upon which the name of the book and its author is engraved.[44]

163
Title-page.
Basinio de'Basini, *Astronomicon*.
Padua, before 1460

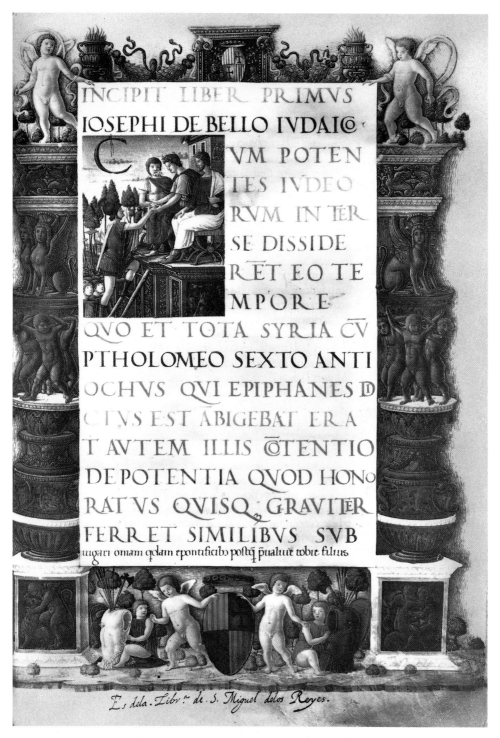

164
Title-page.
Josephus Flavius,
De bello judaico, Book 1.
Lauro Padovano (Padua),
second half of 15th century

IV · Didactic Miniatures

To CAPTURE the essence of medieval illumination and avoid the error of judging it according to our own preconceptions (as though it were monumental art on a smaller scale and a substitute for lost frescoes or panel paintings), we have had to concentrate first on those forms of decoration which are specific to the book and which do not occur in any other form of painting: initials, borders, Canon-table arcading, title-pages and the like. We have already become acquainted with the various procedures developed to integrate pictorial elements into the organism of the book-page, namely, the elevation of script symbols (letters) to the status of representational art, and conversely, the disintegration and metamorphosis of representational art into symbolic signs and ornament. Now, however, we shall take the bull by the horns and enquire into the kind of art that spurns disguise or camouflage in order to achieve its right to exist in the territory of the written word: in short, the *full-page picture* which had been used as book-decoration since late-antique and pre-Carolingian times. What was the nature of its illustrative function in the book? What artistic purpose did it serve?

It must be stressed that this function is not synonymous with, nor should it be confused with the picture as an instrument of the Christian religion. Already in the sixth century, Pope Gregory the Great had formulated the religious function of the picture quite precisely for the Roman Church. In his apologia for pictorial art, contained in a letter to the Bishop of Marseilles, Gregory explains that pictures have a didactic function – they are the Bible and hagiography of the illiterate, communicating to them pictorially, visually, rather than in writing.[32] Naturally this justification would be useless in a Christian world without illiteracy. What is relevant for our problem is something else: book illumination is not the only art-form that carries didactic responsibility – all pictorial art has this function, and in Gregory's time it was chiefly monumental art. Pictorial communication is not solely the domain of the book. The earliest typological art known – where the New Testament is prefigured *ad oculos* by the Old Testament – occurs in monumental art. In illuminated manuscripts, the great vogue for typology is not encountered until the twelfth century.

It is certainly true that the book was the ideal place where didactic art, by the combination of word and picture, could succeed most triumphantly; and moreover, that these pictures could be regarded as

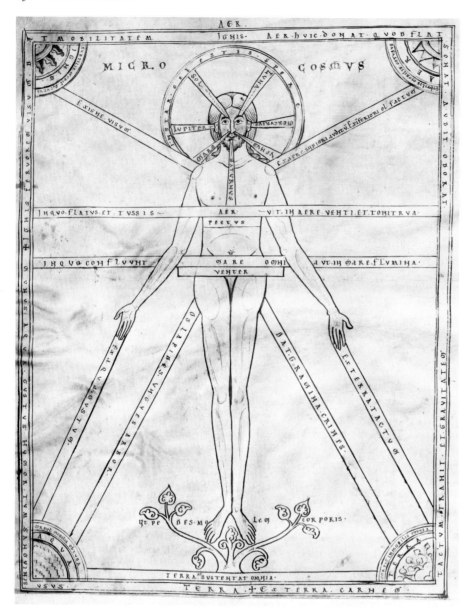

165
Man as microcosm.
Salomo of Constance, Commentary.
Regensburg-Prüfening, 1165

useful teaching aids in the study of theology. In the later Middle Ages, the most complicated philosophical systems were readily represented in pictures, and what we metaphorically describe as a world-view was often literally offered as a picture to be looked at. In a Regensburg manuscript of the twelfth century there is a picture of the microcosm (fig. 165). It is a legacy from an ancient tradition which had its origin in the cosmogony and cosmology of the East, and in which the human form is to be understood as a mirror of the universe. Classical astrology had bequeathed this idea to the Middle Ages as a conceptual structure based on the influence of the stars upon the life of mankind, that is, the influence of macrocosm on microcosm. The Regensburg-Prüfening diagram represents the concordance between parts of the human body and the macrocosm, and is thus a variant on the idea, familiar from the Bible, that man was created in God's image. Man, not Christ, is represented in the diagram – the 'cross-shaped' nimbus is misleading – the rays of light are only there for the inscription. The marginal notes tell us that the feet of man are the earth, his knees stones, his nails trees, his hair grass, his chest air, his stomach the sea, and his head Heaven. One other equation between macrocosm and microcosm should really have been shown in this diagram, namely that in the outstretched arms, the span and height of man are identical, exactly as the dimensions of the world which can thus be circumscribed in a circle. A related miniature of the same date shows this form of microcosm with an equation of the two measurements (fig. 166). In addition, the human figure is here shown in relation to the four elements and the four winds. The Regensburg draughtsman, however, goes further and integrates composition and frame with inscribed bands; the corners of the frame are occupied by the four elements.

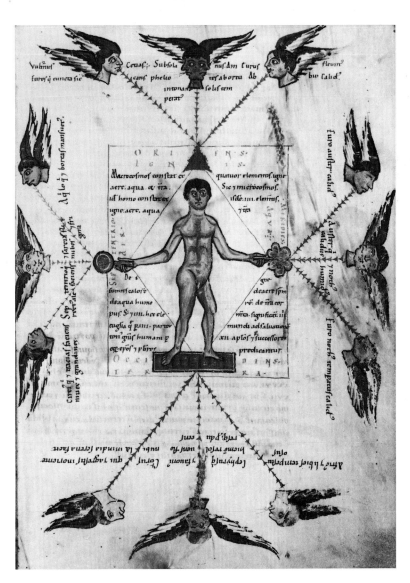

166
Man as microcosm,
with the four elements and wind-gods.
Astronomical Treatise.
Prüfening, third quarter of 12th century

167
The four orders of creation.
Honorius Augustodunensis,
Clavis physicae.
Meuse region (?), mid 12th century

Even more ambitious than this pictorial diagram is a roughly contemporary miniature from the monastery of Michelsberg near Bamberg, which probably had been illuminated in the Meuse region. It illustrates the treatise 'Clavis physicae' (Key to Nature) by Honorius Augustodunensis (fig. 167), which reflects a view of the world in the spirit of Plato taken from one of the greatest medieval Irish philosophers, John Scotus Erigena. The four compartments of the miniature signify the four natures of creation. Uppermost, in a kind of lunette, are the 'primordiales causae', the principles of all things, that which creates but itself has not been created. Following the pattern of Sapientia (divine wisdom) and her seven daughters, the manifestations of Divinity – Justitia, Virtus, Ratio, Veritas, Essentia, Vita and Sapientia – appear as half-figures, gathered around the central and crowned figure of quintessential Bonitas. Below, in the second row, is found the 'effectus causarum', what is created and in its turn creates – as the contents of three medallions: on the left, a personification of Time; on the right, of Space, and in the centre a four-headed conglomerant in a kind of whirl-pattern – unformed matter, according to the inscription. Lower down, 'natura creata', created nature, is seen beneath four arcades: angels, birds, fish, plants, animals and men, the creations which themselves do not form new creations, i.e. formed matter. The lowest register in the shape of a reversed lunette is occupied by the bust of the nimbed God – who holds all threads of the fabric of the universe in his hands. The inscription 'finis' alludes to the words of Honorius Augustodunensis: the Word of God is contained in the beginning and end of all things ('universalis quippe totius creature finis Dei verbum est').[45]

Whether such a pictorial diagram is anything more than a mnemonic – a technique adopted to facilitate an understanding of a hierarchy of abstractions embodied by personifications and symbols – is still an open question. We are closer to 'art' in cases where the ontology offered is not just academic philosophy but a visionary

168
Cosmic vision.
Hildegard von Bingen, *Scivias*.
Southern Germany, c. 1165

revelation, as, for example, in the illustrations of the work of the Rhenish nun Hildegard von Bingen (pl. XXIV). As she indicates in her foreword, her insights have not been reached via other teachings ('de alia doctrina'), but gained along the path of the living light ('per viam vivent is luminis').[46] Hildegard attains her vision of the world not by theological speculation, but rather from spontaneous inspiration. 'The supersensory', as it has been called in a study of her allegories, 'is not pursued by dialectical development, but is established in its essence by a specific embodiment before the eyes'[47] – a theology in pictures. The picture in this instance is not, as it were, a crutch; as visionary inspiration it is the original form of all the complexities of thought, and the painted picture is an attempt to make accessible to the external eye what the inner eye has perceived. This is especially true of illustrations to the Book of Revelation which, as a literary work, is not only the finest of its type but also the specific source for this kind of religious experience.

Even in Hildegard's cosmic vision (fig. 168), much of the content is to be associated with what is not directly accessible to the senses. The large oval with its fiery outer border is supposed to express God's strength 'which vengefully attacks non-believers but is the fire of comfort and purification to believers'.[48] One star in this zone stands for Christ and his burning love; the three stars above, for the Trinity. The winds that fan out from this zone of fire are supposed to be an allegory for the prophecy of God through the sermon. If your eye penetrates from this external zone into the inner reaches of the mandorla-shaped oval, there is first a strip of dark fire, the works of the Devil, then the lighter, star-strewn sphere of the ether of the believer, in the centre of which floats a flaming ball, associated with other bodies of light which symbolize the Church and the two Testaments, its light from the stars of the zone encompassing all.[48] Still many further allegories are worked into the picture for the reader to perceive and to understand.

Hildegard's text is both a vision and a meaningful commentary. The illustrator has attempted to reinterpret the most important visions in her work, but in so doing it was inevitable that his pictures would contain translations of non-visual and purely symbolic elements and that their allegorical-didactic character would be foremost. In short, the miniatures remain for the most part mere curiosities.

V · Illustration of the Apocalypse

THE PROTOTYPE for the mystic vision of the Rhenish nun Hildegard was the Revelation of St. John, banished to Patmos. It too, has a good deal of non-visual material, but in origin it is entirely different: it does not belong to the cold light of theological reason, however much touched by mysticism, but has its roots in the fact that the author of the Apocalypse, John, like the Hebrew prophets before him who wrote the books of Daniel and Enoch, came from a civilization which was essentially devoid of pictures. The heated fantasies of the Apocalypse as a literary genre paid no attention to what was visually possible. It was apparently this abandonment of restraint in spurning a logical point of view, as if in a waking dream or a brainstorm, which stimulated the Middle Ages – characteristically not the Greek East but the Latin West – to compose in pictorial *non-sequiturs*. It is all the more important to investigate the imaginative illogicality of this kind of illustration because it repeatedly produced real picture books of a specifically medieval character and some of the most significant art of the Middle Ages.

From copies made around 800 A.D., we can conclude that the Book of Revelation – a text not recognized by the eastern Church – had already been illustrated in late-antique times. Although this pictorial cycle must have belonged to a phase of severely degenerate classicism, the classical backbone was strong enough to enable the illustrators to make of the metaphysics of St. John's narrative more of an affirmation than a showpiece of the disintegration of the classical innately logical view: this can be seen in the Apocalypses of Cambrai and Trier, which were copied from Early Christian manuscripts (figs. 169, 170).

It was not until about the end of the eighth century that a sequence of illustrations was created that could match the magnitude of the vision: a new commentary on the Apocalypse appeared in Spain, written by Beatus of Liébana. Since only illustrated copies of this work are extant, it may be inferred that from the outset this glossed Apocalypse was produced as a picture book. The example which I shall examine more closely, the Beatus manuscript from Santo Domingo de Silos (pl. XX), comes from a much later date, shortly before 1100; but Mozarabic art – the art of Christian Spain under Arabic rule – tenaciously retained its style almost unchanged for centuries and in this respect is comparable to Irish art, and like it, essentially a manifestation of pre-Carolingian aesthetics.[49] Here, the subject of the miniature is the Adoration of the Lamb by the Twenty-four Elders. It is in fact already the second illustration in the manuscript of the vision in the fourth chapter, obviously inspired by a change of scene in the course of the vision. Illogically, like the visionary John himself, the miniaturist forgets that his subject was the Twenty-four Elders seated around the Throne of God, and he makes half of them encircle a Lamb in a medallion (Rev. 4,4). For the starting point of the illustration, the text is taken from where John sees the Lamb enthroned amidst the four creatures (Zoa), and adored by the Elders – the Lamb, that shall loosen the seal of the Book (Rev. 5,6). The artist saw here an opportunity to create a radial composition which made individual connection to the central figure of the Lamb a decisive factor for all figures, the Elders and the four Zoa, and it ignored such questions as the spatial anchorage of figures on a supporting foundation or base line. One need only glance at the corresponding illustration in the Trier Apocalypse (fig. 170), a copy of an Early Christian Italian work, to grasp immediately the fundamental novelty and specifically medieval character of the pictorial inventiveness that pervades the Spanish manuscript. In the Trier version, the Vision of the Lamb is still wholly cast in the perspective of an onlooker from earth. The Twenty-four Elders stand on the ground; above them hover the angels, and all look up to Heaven above the clouds in which the four winged Zoa flank the *clipeus* with the Lamb. In spite of the eschatological, transcendental nature of the subject, the pictorial and artistic point of view in the Trier Apocalypse is still geocentric: below, Earth; above, Heaven. The pictorial field, although very flattened, is nevertheless an approximation of real space.

The theophany of the Spanish Apocalypse (pl. XX) is both nowhere and everywhere. Every individual figure is placed in an arrangement that emanates from the centre, and such a representational approach can be justifiably regarded as expressing a theocentric view of the world. Even the angels near the lower picture-edge are aligned with the centre of the large wheel of the world, not suspended in airy heights to which we look up. The Almighty in his mandorla, held by angels in flight, crowns the global shape of the world; and placed thus outside the circle, his dominion over creation is thereby symbolized. The original designer of this composition, who was obviously not the miniaturist of the manuscript of Santo Domingo de Silos, and who must have lived more than a century earlier, wished to do justice to the two divine beings, the Lamb and the Christ in Majesty – a kaleidoscopic change in the manifestation of God which the text describes with all the illogicality of a vision: for John tells first of One sitting on the throne (Rev. 5,1), but then, as no one can loosen the seal of the Book, he suddenly speaks of the Lamb in the midst of the throne (Rev. 5,6). The insensitivity to contradictions in the narrative sequence is matched by the illuminator's own disregard for the spatial segregation of Lamb and throned Deity, who are supposed to appear one after the other but in the same place. Time is here translated into space. But this Mozarabic approach is also insensitive to any distinction between stillness and movement. Eight of the Elders stand

169
The Woman and Dragon.
Cambrai Apocalypse.
France, second half of 9th century

170
Adoration of the Lamb.
Trier Apocalypse.
France, first quarter of 9th century

in pairs, arranged radially in the four directions of the winds, while between each pair one figure lies flat – because the text reads: the Elders, as they recognize the Lamb, prostrate themselves (Rev. 5, 8). In so doing the figures of the prostrate Elders reinforce the outer line of the circle at four points, strengthening our inclination to read the whole as a rotating movement. In this sort of composition, it is not the movement of the Elders, nor their prostrating themselves, nor even the circumnavigation of the angels which is illustrated, but the eternal circle of the whole within itself.

All this takes place in the display-space of the book-page, not in an imaginary space, not even in those poor spatial imitations found in medieval copies of late-classical Apocalypse illustrations (figs. 169, 170). The miniature itself creates the page-pattern; its decorative formal function is the primary determinant of its style. Its subject matter calls for a particular choice in the overall form of the pattern, the collective plan, and this in turn dictates the way it is executed down to the last detail. An abstract sense of colour (pl. xx), yellow and red contrasting with brown/black/green for the strongest statements, is the mainstay of the decorative scheme and, in its turn, helps to emphasize the specific meaning of the representation: for example, the red cross formed by the red wings of the four Zoa creates a stabilizing counterforce against the predominant radial movement in the composition. For the patterning to be paramount, as it is, all organic forms must be conceived as insubstantial, in particular the human form, whose drapery provides a convenient pretext for creating a predominantly multi-coloured, anthropomorphic arrangement of stripes. Everything is patterned, every surface, down to the smallest detail – and yet the overall planning and execution may still retain its independent symbolism.

Compared with Spanish Apocalypse illustration, all later treatment of such visionary themes is a compromise with actual visual experience. This is true of the Ottonian Apocalypse whose version of the same subject, the Adoration of the Lamb (fig. 171) offers a scheme of composition no different from that of an Ascension of Christ. And it is no less true of English illustrations from the thirteenth century[50],

171
Christ in Majesty
adored by the 24 Elders.
Bamberg Apocalypse.
Reichenau (?), 1000–1002

172
Christ in Majesty
adored by the 24 Elders.
Lambeth Apocalypse.
English, late 13th century

where the Adoration of the Lamb (fig. 172) already bears the stamp of the Christ in Majesty tympana of Romanesque and early Gothic monumental sculpture (fig. 173), except that the four-cornered format of the book has imposed another arrangement upon the composition than that of the round or pointed arch of the tympanum. The page is divided geometrically into regular compartments, the lower edge of which serves in each case as a base-line for standing or seated figures. It is the alternating coloured background that binds the whole together by the creation of a surface-pattern, in this case a blue/red chequerboard. In later examples of English Apocalypses

173
Christ in Majesty
adored by the 24 Elders.
Moissac, former Abbey Church of Saint-Pierre,
south-door tympanum.
Southern French, 1120–1135

(pl. XXV), the representation of the vision has changed to one primarily seen in the form of light. Curious as it may seem, pictorial fantasy has been ignited from its own verbal source. Visions are in themselves an 'enlightenment', in its literal meaning, and the figurative language of the New Testament is full of descriptions of optic phenomena like the fall of hail (Rev. 16, 20) or the rain of fire and ashes mixed with blood (Rev. 8, 7), or burning mountains which plunge into the sea (Rev. 8, 8), or the rainbow which hovers over the head of an angel whose face is the sun and whose feet are pillars of fire (Rev. 1, 15 ff.), and similar luminary occurrences. The early Spanish Apocalypse (pl. XX) used, in all its pictures, ground colours with ecstatic tones – sulphur yellow and carmine – but it was never concerned with the depiction of specific light, except in such cases where, for instance, blood and fire is to be represented, and the ground is shown to be blood-red. English pictorial cycles from the end of the thirteenth century were the first to attempt to capture the atmosphere of the narrative, and to make that the essence of the picture. In this they anticipate developments in modern art, though naturally not without imbuing colour-values with rhythmic and formalized ornamental qualities.

VI · Illustration of the Psalter

BESIDES THE APOCALYPSE, there was still another text which, with its symbolic language, galvanized the pictorial fantasy of the illuminator into action: the Psalter[51]. I am referring here only to those Psalter illustrations which follow that distinctive and profoundly medieval system of illustrating 'the Word'. The rich pictorial language of the Psalter is not that of a visionary, of someone in a trance, in a waking dream, as was the Apocalypse. It depends rather on an inexhaustible fund of inventiveness and on an extravagantly tireless use of metaphor, which renders visible essentially abstract concepts like the power, glory, magnitude, goodness, omniscience of the Creator, trust in God, or the sinfulness, iniquity, wickedness of evil; and it aims to make these concepts physically comprehensible. The oriental rhetoric of the 'author' of the Psalms – it is well-known that the Psalms of David are the work of several authors – overleaps the boundaries of all levels of meaning and by poetic licence says much which in ordinary daily speech would be little more than false comparison. The language strikes us as strange because of the emphasis on simile and the way the thing compared from one sphere is placed in tandem with its analogue, for example, when it is said, 'Out of the mouth of babes and sucklings hast thou ordained strength' (Psalm 7, 3) or, 'They speak loftily. They set their mouth against the heavens and their tongue walketh through the earth' (Psalm 72,8 f.). The medieval artist, however, found this language congenial and reacted in a surprising way to it.

A good deal of the vocabulary of all language is figurative, and in daily use it is understood as such. If someone says, 'My lips are sealed', no one is going to examine his mouth for signs of sealing wax. In fact, the statement could not have been uttered at all if what was said had been literally true. Moreover, no one who reads the verse, 'The righteous put forth their hands unto iniquity' (Psalm 124, 3) will normally attempt to visualize these hands. But this is precisely the kind of abstruse idea that was hit upon in the Middle Ages: numerous psalms were read not in a metaphorical sense but literally, that is, *au pied de la lettre*. And in transferring the 'word picture' into the illustration intact, verbal imagery became visual imagery.

This often had curious results. For instance, a Byzantine illuminator illustrates the aforementioned description of the proud man by taking the figurative language in sections – first a mouth reaching to Heaven and then a tongue dropping to the ground (Psalm 72,9; fig. 174) –

or when Mercy is shown as almsgiver on whose head are sprouting branches (fig. 175), because he is 'the righteous, who flourishes green as the palm tree, he waxes like the cedars in Lebanon' (Psalm 91, 13). Today we still use the idiom of someone 'flourishing'; but we understand it in an abstract sense. The actual image has long been lost and the expression is merely an echo of a forgotten metaphor. The illuminator's relationship to the word, in these instances, is either that he is conscious of its original symbolic meaning or has only just become aware of it. It is often said that medieval art is abstract. However, although here the subject matter to be depicted is abstract – virtue and vice, for example – the essence of the representational technique is a literal embodiment of the abstraction.

What happens when figurative language, which has become hackneyed through usage, is taken absolutely seriously, can be seen in Bruegel's illustration of Proverbs,[52] where, for example, 'banging one's head against the wall' or 'casting pearls before swine' is depicted literally. What Bruegel has painted is a striking example of word illustration. However, his is not entirely the same as the medieval approach, because there is another dimension to his composition, and that is the comic nature of word pictures if taken seriously. Bruegel has put himself in the position of an innocent and acts as if he believes every word literally; and in this way he shows human activity and behaviour in all its absurdity and exposes its innate insanity. Medieval word illustration, however, is not a tool of humour or of social satire. The medieval mind took the word seriously and therefore *eo ipso* the picture created from it. Seen from this point of view, we can say rather that the 'word picture' contains not insanity but genuine truth. Medieval man believed that he could gain insights from word illustration, that he could discover hidden meanings in the word. He was etymologically oriented. And therefore, in trying to represent abstract concepts, the medieval illuminator, rather than interpreting words symbolically, depicts them literally.

Byzantine marginal miniatures, from which our examples of word illustration have so far been taken, represent only one of several methods used in the illustration of the Psalter. In the western world, this kind of design was reapplied repeatedly to produce whole cycles of Psalter illustrations. The most outstanding representative of this type is unquestionably the Carolingian Psalter, today at Utrecht, illuminated in the third decade of the ninth century at Reims. The pictorial quotations from the Psalter text are not scattered haphazardly across the margins of the pages, as in Byzantine examples, but integrated into extensive landscape 'scenarios', in which series of single episodes create a kind of unity. However, even in this, the Carolingian draughtsman had Byzantine precursors.[53] One must bear in mind that the psalms do not tell a coherent story, that mood and metaphor follow one another in a flood of ideas in rapid sequence; in short, that the individual psalms have, if any, only a purely conceptual unity. The artist or artists of the Utrecht Psalter allowed themselves to be

174
Illustration to Psalm 72.
Psalter. Illuminated by Theodorus
in the Monastery of Studios, 11th century

175
Illustration to Psalm 91.
Psalter. Illuminated by Theodorus
in the Monastery of Studios, 11th century

176
Illustration to Psalm 68.
Utrecht Psalter. Reims, c. 830

stimulated by the occasional motif or verbal image that occurred in this loose chain of ideas; and in depicting them they provided a synopsis for these unconnected pictorial motifs by using them to fill broad landscape vistas. The illusionistic landscape, inherited from the Antique, is analogous to the unfettered space in which the psalmist's sense and sensibility roam restlessly.[54]

There is no definite order in which to read these pictures; the sequence of thoughts and ideas is amorphous in order to fit the logical point of view of an illusionary space. Scenes with water, stream or sea, are placed below; what takes place above on a mountain or in the heavenly spheres, has naturally to appear at the top of the picture and then, to separate what might be closely related images, individual scenes are set in the middle zone, illustrating episodes which in fact may only occur in much later verses. In the well known psalm, a prayer for rescue from the depths of the waters, which reads, 'Salvum me fac ...' (Psalm 68) – later usually illustrated in concise form by David, naked but crowned, supplicating from the water (fig. 150) – one finds in the Utrecht Psalter right at the bottom of the illustration, a shipwrecked man with outstretched arms calling on the Lord for help (fig. 176); he could be speaking the opening words of the verse, 'Save me, O God; for the waters are come in unto my soul'. The Lord, however, is too busy to hear him: passing judgement, He instructs one of two scribes to remove someone from the Book of the Living; this 'someone' refers to the enemies of the psalmist pleading for help, an episode which is not recounted until verse 29 of the psalm. And the same water which threatens to engulf the shipwrecked man of verse 1, is about to swallow up guests at a banquet, described in verse 23. The illuminator first thought of this combination because he had the water with the shipwrecked man at his disposal. We see that what may have absolutely no connection in the flow of ideas,

may well find itself in closest contact in the continuum of a landscape setting; indeed, as in the case of the banqueting scene, it can produce completely new motifs which are not at all to be found in the text of the psalm.

There appears to be no rule whatsoever about what or how much of a psalm's text was 'quoted' or used, nor how intensively or extensively single episodes would be illustrated. Psalms with a wealth of verses can be illustrated by merging a few pictorial motifs and, conversely, fairly short psalms can give rise to multi-episodic illustration. In the illustration of Psalm 11 (pl. XVIII, figs. 10, 11), two groups of figures are distinguished by their unusual activity. One group is moving around an object similar to a round table-top or a pane of glass; the other is turning a capstan and keeping it in rotation. In both episodes there is the same meaning, namely that 'the sinner goes around in circles' (in circuitu impii ambulant ..., Psalm 11,9), that is, they make no headway. One point in the text has here given rise to two illustrations. The famous verse about the hart who thirsteth for the waters as the soul of the believer for God (Psalm 41,1), most often represented in the Middle Ages by a hart drinking water and by the psalmist who indicates with one hand the hart as symbolizing his soul and with the other the Hand of God (fig. 15), this the Utrecht Psalter illustrates quite superficially in a tiny scene of a wild deer harassed by hounds (fig. 177); on the other hand, the words of the psalmist's enemies, 'who now that he lieth he shall rise up no more' (Psalm 40,9), remind the illustrator immediately of the Ascension of Christ, according to the interpretation of the New Testament, and is for him an excuse to draw the Holy Sepulchre and not far from it the encounter of the Risen Christ with the two Marys (fig. 178). This is no longer 'word illustration' in the narrower sense but the visualizing of word-associations. What is strange, however, is that the same illustrator who conveys the true prophetic sense of the psalms, that is, interprets them in a typological and allegorical manner, often reverts to the most naïve word illustration, as for example in Psalm 43 which contains the verse, 'Awake, why sleepest thou, O Lord?' (verse 23). We see a four-poster bed with canopy on which God is resting (fig. 179).

The many classicizing personifications of natural elements, such as Terra, River-Gods, the Heavenly Bodies, Hades and other classical motifs (fig. 180), which appear throughout the Utrecht Psalter, raise the possibility – indeed make it certain – that these Carolingian miniatures are based on an Early Christian model, and that they had found there an already fully developed system of word illustration. That the Carolingian draughtsmen, however, have copied slavishly from their model, and can therefore lay no claim whatsoever to the originality of the pictorial conception, seems more than unlikely. First of all, there are no grounds (and we know this from late-antique book illustration) for the view that Early Christian Psalter illustrations were executed in an outline style such as practised at Reims. We cannot assume that already in Early Christian times the illusionistic style of late-classicism had been translated and reinterpreted into the graphic,

177-179
Illustrations to Psalms 41, 40 and 43 (details).
Utrecht Psalter. Reims, c. 830

180
Illustration to Psalm 92 (detail).
Utrecht Psalter. Reims, c. 830

sketch-like language which for us constitutes much of the originality of the pictures of the Utrecht Psalter, and whose linearity exercised
so profound an influence on Anglo-Saxon (fig. 180 a) and later English
work (fig. 185). The sketchy graphics of this style have an eminently
illustrative and at the same time a most un-classical function, namely
a pictorial equivalent for the lightning-like flash and play of thoughts,
images and moods of the poet. This style of drawing makes it possible
to pen the pictures evoked at hearing the psalms as an accompaniment
similarly produced at lightning speed. The extraordinary excitement
which grips figures and landscape with equal intensity, so that everything appears to vibrate, is one of the most important factors of the
Psalter's pictorial unity; it is an excitement which, all-encompassing,
cannot be an external phenomenon, and which in a most remarkable
way conveys the passionate inner state of the psalmist to the viewer
of the inspired illustrations. The picture here is a veritable seismograph
which registers the excitement of religious ecstasy. To read and to
observe here is the same thing, and that is probably what is specifically
medieval in the grandiose draughtsmanship of the Utrecht Psalter.

180 a
Illustration to Psalm 118 (detail).
Utrecht Psalter Copy.
Anglo-Saxon, c. 1000

VII · The Conflict of Surface and Space: an Ongoing Process

IN AN EARLIER CHAPTER we discussed purely decorative initials and ligatures of letters which appear to us just like pictures, and are even framed individually like pictures – in fact, script as illustration (pls. III, IX, XIV, XV, figs. 40, 89 ff.). In didactic pictures, as in Psalters, where word illustration is the intention, we find miniatures in which the combination and juxtaposition of pictorial elements (that is, the composition) clearly derives from the syntax of language – the structure of verbally formulated sequences of thought. These are pictures 'written' as verbal statements, and as a result need to be understood by being 'read' rather than by being simply looked at. The possibility of juxtaposing the two phenomena – the visual display aspect of the script and the 'readability' of the pictorial components – is a specifically medieval feature. Symbiosis of script and picture is another aspect of the same phenomenon. Earlier, we looked at stages in this symbiosis where the picture was an alien element accommodated by the script – the figure initial, historiated initial and related forms. We will now look at a reversal of that relationship, at cases where the picture is host and the script guest (this does not, of course, apply where the text is simply a marginal inscription).

The Lindisfarne Gospels, a major work of Insular art of the late seventh century, affords excellent examples. The frontispiece to each Gospel shows the Evangelist with his attribute, the animal symbol by which the authorship of the text can be recognized (fig. 181). But for the Insular artist this alone was not a sufficiently strong indication of the transcendental import of the picture: he felt a need also to inscribe the picture. In appropriate gradation, he wrote, in Greek, the name of the Evangelist in monumental pseudo-Greek characters, and that of the animal symbol in smaller Roman letters in Latin, decoratively spaced within the interior of the picture. The eye moves from picture to symbol and from symbol to script by stages. This is a kind of 'speaking' picture, which claims our attention simultaneously at different levels, just as the modern poster does with picture, emblem and script.

A prerequisite for this symbiosis is that the field of action is the same for viewing as for reading – the same substratum for picture and script, each being applied flat to the bare surface of the page. Both elements – picture and script, appear on what must be entirely

181
St. Luke.
Lindisfarne Gospels. Insular, before 698 (?)

neutral space; it is not an imagined continuum of space, nor one that is either two- or three-dimensional. In Early Christian examples, individual subjects occupied illusionistic pictorial space; but in the Lindisfarne Gospels these images seem like isolated cut-outs stuck on to the page. There is no general base-line for figures or objects, only the surface of the page on which images and letters are to be placed in more or less loose groupings.

Besides these full-page pictures, Insular books also have pages densely decorated with purely ornamental patterns and framed similarly as full-page miniatures – the so-called carpet pages (pl. IV). Herein lies the second characteristic of the early-medieval book-page: its function as decoration. Even full-page pictures (figs. 181, 182) are fundamentally organized as patterned pages. In general, to be assimilated into the organism of the book and its decoration, representational subjects have to undergo a rigorous ornamentalization – what is characterized by the much abused word 'stylization'. The object of this exercise is to refine natural forms – which we have a tendency to regard as barbarisms; and the elements seen as 'formless' to primitive man (or rather, to those accustomed to abstract fantasy), are refined with ornament consisting of well-established forms such as ribbon patterns

182
St. John.
Gospels. Insular, 8th century

for drapery, spirals for hair or volutes for beard strands, circles for pupils, delta forms for ears and so forth (pl. v, figs. 181, 182). In this way, calligraphy is created out of – to primitive eyes – apparently raw or unsightly 'nature'. It must be pointed out in this context, that during the period under discussion scribe and miniaturist were frequently one and the same person, that is to say, script, decoration and picture were executed by one man;[55] this helps to explain why reading and looking at this level can be accomplished within one act of viewing.

This tendency towards ornament, as briefly indicated, is symptomatic of an assimilation process in which organic-representational form succumbs to the imperatives of the principles of page decoration. Participants in pictorial space now become part of a pictorial pattern and, in the course of this process, both independent organic existence and the requirements of objective reality have to be sacrificed to the laws of the picture-pattern and of page design. The human figure stiffens into a fossilized figure-pattern with, at times, no higher status than an anthropomorphic emblem. The entire subsequent development of medieval illumination can now be seen as a conflict of two systems of expression in which there is an attempt to shed the constraints of abstract pattern, to affirm the logic of palpable reality where possible without, however, having to relinquish the benefits of an abstract formal arrangement with its inherent transcendental meaning. Somewhat simplistically, the clash can be understood as a conflict of the two constituent legacies of the Middle Ages, the barbarian (Mediterranean as well as northern) and the Mediterranean-classical tradition, and so in the following pages I should like to sketch briefly the most important stages in the resolution of this conflict.

It is now generally accepted, despite some earlier doubts, that the division of medieval art history into periods essentially follows the rhythm of the most significant advances in, and attempts at, reviving the classical tradition – the individual rivulets, as it were, which fed the broad stream of development and which we characterize as Renaissance movements: the Carolingian Renaissance, preceded in the pre-Carolingian period by a Renaissance in Northumbria and southern England (more than fifty years earlier, about mid eighth century), and which had an Anglo-Saxon sequel in the tenth and eleventh centuries; then the parallel artistic manifestation of the Ottonian *Renovatio Imperii Romani*; next, the revival efforts of the Romanesque, which chose as its lodestar the art of contemporary Byzantium, the medieval heir of the Antique; and finally, the Gothic period. The Gothic wears a Janus face. On the one hand, its immediate successors in the post-medieval Renaissance, the first truly triumphant Renaissance in every respect, scathingly called it 'Barbarian' (after the vandals that gave the Roman world the death-blow); while, on the other hand, it has long since been re-evaluated as the forerunner of the 'modern' world – one need only think of the emancipation of sculpture in the round. It is this aspect of the Gothic, particularly in

France, its proper birthplace, that has earned it the accolade *humanisme gothique*. To be historically accurate, we must not lose sight of this double-sided nature of the Gothic, which Max Dvořák expressed in the title of his well-known study 'Idealismus und Naturalismus in der gothischen Skulptur und Malerei'.[56]

At the beginning of Renaissance movements, in every case, there is a phase of intense receptivity to classical models, an embrace of classical ideals and forms of expressions – most uninhibitedly so in the Carolingian Renaissance. In this period the admired past is openly copied (fig. 183), without any embarrassment in reproducing a model exact in every detail, so much so that the Carolingian illuminator is occasionally able to deceive modern critics into believing they have a late-antique original before them. Also with a number of ivories, as is well known, the question as to whether they are antique originals or Carolingian copies is still open.[57] There are instances where something specifically medieval betrays itself in some minor detail of which the Carolingian copyist may not even have been aware. And where the Carolingian painter does not confine himself to the role of mere copying, then the distinctive contribution and character of the re-fashioning of the classical pictorial tradition is quite unmistakable.

Two points can be raised here. The first concerns the relationship of frame to inner picture. In the oldest and most classical Evangelist portraits, those of the Vienna Coronation Gospels, the illusion of a framed panel painting is still aspired to (pl. VI). The frame, decorated with botanical ornament, seems to project forward in relief, and through this 'carved' frame one looks into a very painterly picture, one filled with light and air and with a landscaped background, in other words, illusionistic space. In this example, however, something seems to have happened: the foot-stool of John's throne juts out from the pictorial space and cuts across the frame. The Carolingian illuminator seems no longer to have had a clear idea of the difference between the real world and the imagined pictorial space that is separated from the 'real' by a frame. For him, the frame and the interior of the picture are in the same dimension as the book-page.

Some twenty years later, Evangelist portraits were painted at Reims which clearly carried the classically-resonant pictorial language of the Coronation Gospels forward into the Middle Ages (fig. 184). Everything visible – figures, lectern, landscape, but also frame – is transfigured in vibrant movement, as if engulfed by a storm. The motion is at its strongest, its most frenetic, in drapery. In antique art, the form of clothing, the fall of folds, was always used as a device for expressing body movement, the living substance. Here, the vibrating folds of drapery, surging and seething, are filled with an independent dramatic life which obviously has infected even the surrounding lifeless matter. This trembling and fluttering movement – a linear equivalent of the shimmer of illusionistic atmosphere – takes place on the surface of the page, not within the pictorial space. Like the drawings of the Utrecht Psalter (figs. 10, 176-180) from the same

183
St. Matthew and St. Mark.
Gospels from Xanten (detail).
Court School of Charlemagne,
early 9th century

184
St. Matthew.
Ebbo Gospels.
Reims, c. 816-835

Reims atelier, the visible hyper-agitation of line must be understood as a direct transposition, an externalization of an inner excitement, even ecstasy, experienced by the viewer. In a way, this may be seen as an example of medieval expressionism, a kind of medieval antecedent of Van Gogh. The comparison, which can only be made with careful reservations, is nevertheless not wholly misleading because, even in the paintings of Van Gogh, it is the translation into line of originally impressionistic pictorial material which lies at the heart of its expressionism.

The idea of exemplifying or expressing outwardly, through objects of perception, the inner emotions arising during artistic creation, was general practice in the Middle Ages, on both a narrower and a broader level. In it a way was found to give a certain formal independence to objects taken from reality without dissolving them into ornament as in pre-Carolingian art, but at the same time to impart to them a non-organic turbulence which cast a quasi-ornamental unity over the whole. Two levels of meaning functioned simultaneously, an earthly and a metaphysical.

The direct continuation and elaboration of the Reims outline style is to be found in Anglo-Saxon illumination of the tenth and eleventh centuries; but here the wonderful equilibrium of the two factors mentioned above is commuted into an over-emphasis on transcendental dynamism (fig. 185). The movement conveyed in the outline of the figures alters their proportions; soaring upwards, it evaporates the figures' substance. This expressionism finds its counterpart in colour which is fluorescent and irridescent, and in which, often with surprising empathy, the colour of the mood becomes dominant, passing to the object represented: for example, the pale reddish-yellow of Resurrection morning (pl. XIX) or the reddish flickering light of Pentecost.[58] This represents an awareness of the effects of light that one would hardly expect to find in a non-naturalistic style. Even ornament is caught up in the same turbulence of form and colour.

Anglo-Saxon illumination is a late flowering of Carolingian art; in it the assimilation of classical elements into a medieval hierarchy, already begun by the Carolingians, was carried to its logical conclusion, long after Carolingian art itself had died in its continental places of origin, in France and in the Rhineland. Notable achievements in page design were now to be found in English illumination, as had happened once before in the pre-Carolingian period. Its significant contributions to the ornamentation and re-valuation of script have already been discussed. The process I want to look at now, briefly, is that of the new distribution of the picture 'inventory' which, instead of being anchored gravitationally on a base-line, has to strive for the weight that would bring its component parts into harmony with the balance of a *surface pattern*. In practice, this means in many cases a move from the horizontal format inherited from the antique model to a vertical format, in which the main accents of the composition have to be shifted from a picture half the height.

185
Christ Triumphant.
Psalter. Anglo-Saxon,
second quarter of 11th century

The first signs of such a new approach to gravity in pictorial space
is found in the development of Carolingian art. The Evangelist John
in the Soissons Gospels (pl. X), one of the major books from the Court
School of Charlemagne (previously known as the Ada School), sits
on a huge throne-like structure; but it would be difficult to say what
this heavy piece of furniture is supposed to rest on. The throne is
surrounded by a recess or *exedra* lined with windows, which in turn
is framed by a rounded archway, through which, as it were, the vista
is seen. This – the Evangelist sitting in a niche under an arcade – has
a long history going back to late-antique author-portraits and pictures
of enthroned consuls. The seated dignitary is placed, like an *homme-*

186
Baptism of Christ.
Ethelwold Benedictional.
Anglo-Saxon, Winchester, 971-984

arcade, in the opening of a space-filled shell, and something of this niche-like character, this indentation of space, still clings to the architectural framework of the picture of St. Luke in the Gospels of St. Augustine in Cambridge, a late-antique Italian production (fig. 36). The St. John picture in the Soissons Gospels is based on an eastern Christian, not an Italian model, with the *exedra* foreshortened in perspective (as in a Byzantine Evangelist picture of the tenth century, fig. 3). The background of the Carolingian picture is like an optical puzzle – one can see the drapery as either convex or concave. The reason for this ambiguity is in fact the diagonal position of the throne: its side-view runs along the left side of the niche, while the front extends into the right wall of the *exedra*. As a result the surface, like a membrane that bends inwards and outwards, is established as the plane of the picture. Another area of ambiguity is the lunette-shaped space containing the eagle symbol: here the upper part can only be viewed as a flat surface, while the lower area also appears as three-dimensional space. But perhaps the most important change from the earlier classical model is in the anchoring of the Evangelist and his throne in the background architecture rather than on the ground. The throne appears to be swept along by the base-line of the *exedra,* the Evangelist floating in mid air. The properties of space help in this case to overcome the weight of material masses.

Finally, partly by way of conclusion and partly to suggest another viewpoint, I should like to mention some of the most important ideas that influenced and motivated the development of book-illumination since the Carolingian period. As already pointed out, the process of eliminating the pictorial orientation inherited from the Antique and shifting it to a different point of gravity within the picture – (a process begun in the Carolingian Renaissance) was brought to completion by Anglo-Saxon illumination of the tenth and eleventh centuries, still using the approach adopted by the Carolingians. Take one of many examples: the Baptism of Christ in the Benedictional of St. Ethelwold (fig. 186) is based on a Carolingian composition preserved in the carving of an ivory casket from Metz (fig. 187), which in turn, judging by its personifications of Nature, is of classical origin. In the course of being turned into a miniature in a book, nothing found in the ivory carving was excluded, not even the pagan personification of the river Jordan, who empties his urn to form the waters of the river. On the Metz casket, however, the scene was treated as a horizontal frieze composition. The transfer to the Benedictional page meant a change from a wide to a tall format, and the illuminator solves the problem in this instance by introducing, above and below, horizontal strips of cloud and water. Only in this way could he fill the entire height of the pictorial field as dictated by the format of the picture. At first this may appear a rather superficial modification of the model to fit the changed proportion of format, perhaps even an attempt at a baroque-like heightening of illusionistic space. In fact, it

187
Baptism of Christ.
Ivory casket (front panel).
Metz, 9th-10th century

188
The Three Marys at the Tomb.
Ethelwold Benedictional.
Anglo-Saxon, Winchester, 971-984

is more than that: it represents a reshaping founded on the principles of a fundamentally different aesthetic. The broad frieze of the Carolingian Baptism is anchored on an imaginary base-line, exactly as in a classical composition. Furthermore, the decorative frame of the ivory establishes an absolute limit for the pictorial field. For the Anglo-Saxon illuminator both these structural rules have lost their validity; for him, the frame represents no inviolable barrier bounding the picture. And since he allows his compositional elements to invade the border and cut across the frame, the scene is, at the same time, pegged upon a scaffold rather than weighted on a base-line or ground surface. The result is to subordinate pictorial narrative to decorative design. Like the Evangelist in the Soissons Gospels (pl. X), a whole scene is here suspended contrary to all laws of earthly gravitation. The page is oriented on a vertical axis; page balance takes priority over the requirement of spatial illusion. If we pursue this development a stage further with another subject, that of the Three Marys at the Tomb (fig. 188), we can see how the original pictorial cohesion progressively

189
The Three Marys at the Tomb.
Benedictional of Robert of Jumièges.
Winchester, c. 980

disintegrates. The horizontal middle-axis upon which the scene is organized is binding – there is no base-line. In a slightly later example (fig. 189), the verticality of the book's format is still more outspoken, with the result that there is no longer room beside the tomb for the guards and they have to serve the other figures as footstools. Individual pictorial elements have thus been re-distributed freely; and where they are used to organize the surface of the page, they tend to be demoted to functionaries in a further process of abstraction. (In a still later miniature, the guards have been completely omitted, fig. 190).

190
The Three Marys at the Tomb.
Psalter. Anglo-Saxon,
Winchester, c. 1050

Contemporary Ottonian illumination, in the late tenth and early eleventh centuries, began to place the conflict between decoration and narrative pictorial claims on an entirely different footing. Efforts were made to escape both from the rigid patterning of the page as well as from the spatial demands of late-antique Carolingian illusionism. To take the latter point first, in Ottonian illumination the continuous but vague illusionistic space is now replaced by stratified space (fig. 191). The cumulative effect produced is one of parallel, flat layers, projected one upon another in extremely thin strata, which appear densely compacted and through which no air may circulate. Differentiation between the layers partly covering one another is established by means of colour; a linear outline of the figures against the ground would have left them amorphous and insubstantial. But Ottonian figures have no outlines; Ottonian drawing or under-drawing is almost non-existent. Only the background has a life of its own,

191
Gregory and his scribe.
'Registrum Gregorii', single leaf.
Master of the 'Registrum Gregorii', Trier, c. 984

192
Crucifixion.
Gospels. Echternach,
mid 11th century

because it has its own abstractly coloured identity set against the smaller islands of colour represented by the figures or the *mise en scène*.

In the mature period of Ottonian painting, the amorphous atmospheric fluidity of Carolingian painting has been totally banished by light purple or pure gold surfaces (pl. XIII), two transcendental colours, which should be understood to represent idealized colours rather than idealized space. Jantzen has spoken of the non-spatiality of Ottonian painting.[59] In its later development, however, Ottonian painting did progress to a kind of coloured panelling, by covering the main figures or groups of figures with separate coloured foil. Gone is the uniform background against which gestures reverberate in broad emptiness. In a Crucifixion from a Gospels made at Echternach (fig. 192), about mid eleventh century, there are rectangular panels of gold singled out behind the figures of Mary and John on the coloured ground of the picture, as if each figure had its own aura. The broad band of the cross serves as foil for the Crucified Christ, and thus the picture seems geometrically divided, parcelled off.

In some Ottonian Schools, for example Regensburg, similarly motivated tendencies led to the dismantling of the total reality of a picture into compartments strictly separated from one another. With this aspect, we come to the second point, the new design of the picture pattern as such.

193
Christ crowning the Emperor Henry II.
Sacramentary of Henry II.
Regensburg, 1002–1014

In the Sacramentary of Henry II (fig. 193), in the miniature showing the Coronation of the Emperor, or more precisely, Christ's blessing of the Emperor – the picture is the fullest embodiment of the idea of rule by God's grace – each of the six figures is assigned a separate field. This 'parcelling' (created mainly by bands of inscription and ornamental strips) is especially striking because the different sections of background have been painted in blue, olive-green and violet. However, at certain points, the figures overstep the boundaries of their compartments and enter adjacent zones (for example, the Emperor obtrudes into the area of Christ's mandorla). In contrast to the static background structure, the slightest change of position in the strata of figures has the effect of a powerful movement.

In this two-fold layering, an essential structural principle of Romanesque page decoration is anticipated as early as the year 1000. It concerns the tectonic structuring of the picture itself as well as of the page. In various ateliers of Romanesque illumination, in different countries, this was achieved in diverse ways; in some, for example in German illumination, there was an unmistakable tendency to submit the human figure to architectural structures, to enclose figures within blocked areas. The English variant is especially interesting, because there the idea is conceived of a tautly organized background and framing zone, (the whole in its turn then appears enclosed in a collage type of frame), to give rise to the development of a totally new narrative style. Among the miniatures in a Life of St. Edmund (fig. 194), a manuscript from the second quarter of the twelfth cen-

194
Glorification of St. Edmund.
Life of St. Edmund.
Bury St. Edmunds,
second quarter of 12th century

tury, there is one which can be recognized as a free paraphrase of the Ottonian Coronation picture from the previous century. It depicts the Glorification of the Martyr King – that is, not an actual but an imagined Coronation. In the Regensburg manuscript, Christ himself crowns the annointed head; in the English miniature the Martyr receives the crown, sceptre and palm from angels. The two large angels flanking Edmund exactly replace the two saints supporting the Emperor and presenting him to God in the Ottonian miniature. In both cases the Coronation is found to be a celebratory showpiece of the crowned figure.

Ceremonial action tends *per se* to an hieratic frontality. A glance at other illustrations of the same subject or related ones, however, shows that in the new manner of English painting, the hieratic note is a factor of the style and not of the subject-matter. In actual pictures of events, in scenes which are supposed to narrate actions and events, and thus are transitory, it is the decorative panelling of the background which makes the frontal appeal to the observer. A picture from the same manuscript contains the scene in which the coffin of the saint is carried across a bridge into the Monastery of Bury St. Edmund's (pl. XXI). Although the action unrolls from left to right, the scene is oriented frontally by means of a division, a parcelling, of the pictorial field. The panelling of the background has given decorum to the scene, the reference to a higher, transcendental order which completely frees the figures for narrative action and the requirements of the objective situation. Since the onus of imparting decorum and organizing the surface pattern of the picture is removed from the figures in the composition, they can fulfil their scenic responsibilities on a scale hitherto impossible and rise wholly to the roles they have to play. We see action and movement in the picture unwind from one side to the other, but we experience the composition, as it were, as entirely frontal. In the School of St. Albans, where this new narrative style was born – and it is a truly narrative style[60] – this is particularly well expressed by one obvious device: without detracting from the frontal orientation of the composition, individual figures are represented almost exclusively in pure profile, that is in the direction in which they are involved in the action; frontal stabilization of the composition is given over entirely to the background (fig. 130).

One important presupposition of the new dramatic possibilities of pictorial narrative has not yet been mentioned: the influence on Romanesque painting of the direct heir of Antiquity, contemporary Byzantine art, and the revival of Christian iconography from that source. Romanesque painting was not the first to turn to Byzantium; it had predecessors in Ottonian illumination from c. 1000. In this respect, even Romanesque art is a kind of Renaissance movement, a Renaissance however, which sprang not from a classicism that was extinct, but from one that was alive. The Entombment miniature of the St. Albans Psalter (fig. 195) shows knowledge of the most recent iconographic re-interpretation in Byzantine art (fig. 196), in which the physical act of burial is turned into a lamentation for the Dead Christ, expressed as Mary's last embrace of her dead son. The note

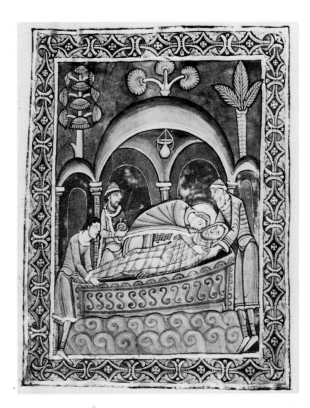

195
Entombment.
St. Albans Psalter.
St. Albans, c. 1119-1123

196
Entombment
(detail from a page with four scenes).
Gospels. Constantinople,
second half of 11th century

struck here is that of the spiritual poetry earlier intoned in the '*Planctus Mariae*'. Now, under the impulse of new religious sentiment, which meant an identification and sympathy with the emotions of the saintly and the holy, a revolution began in Christian art. It led first to a *humanizing* of all that was sacred, but then to a *secularization* which eventually brought the existence of religious art itself into question: for it led inexorably to physical embodiment and that implied taking the magic from mystery. Let us pursue just one aspect in the development of this process of progressive visualization of the events of salvation, the principal subject-matter of religious pictorial art. To visualize every incident in that sequence of events was not possible without first taking a stand on the question of its localization, without defining the 'when' and especially the 'where' more precisely. This again raised new questions about the status of the picture itself, and that of the individual pictorial elements as part of the decoration of the page. In medieval illumination, every pictorial subject had two loyalties: it had to function decoratively as a part of the organized page-surface, and at the same time establish its credibility as participant in a scenario. When the latter function was subjected to a process of spatialization, it was inevitable that the two loyalties would come into open conflict.

197
Prophet Isaiah.
Commentary on Isaiah.
Normandy, late 11th century

The seeds of this conflict – which I would like to call the clash of two domains – were sown in the Romanesque period. At that time, alongside panelled backgrounds, a second form of structured patterning made its appearance: narrative scenes are given an architectural background, an architectural setting which only partly serves to localize the event depicted; it is mostly used as a rhythmic device. The architecture is there to establish the right gaps and links between the figures, and thus to make clear the dramatic meaning of the composition. At a time when architecture was the leading art-form, it was only too easy to borrow from it formulae that would help in the design of the page. Here we have an eloquent example of dual loyalties: an architectural motif can belong to the internal content of the picture to indicate locality, but at the same time function as part of the architectural patterning of the page itself.

Yet another form of page design with architectural elements gained more general validity: it was the use of architecture as a frame, that is situated outside the picture. In a Norman manuscript, a Commentary on Isaiah (fig. 197), the frontispiece shows the prophet in strong frontal pose, seated under an arch that is decorated with complex architectural baldachin-forms, a mass of turrets, arched galleries, roofs and various other forms of Church architecture. What this is supposed to illustrate is less the monumentality of any particular building than the majesty of *Ecclesia* as a general concept. Occasionally architectural structures also had been used in Anglo-Saxon illumination, not only for the Canon Tables (a task for which they were suited), but for example also for the framing of Evangelist portraits. But nowhere was the framing arch ever burdened to such an extent with domes as it is in the massive upper structures of Norman miniatures around the year 1100. Forerunners of this type of architectural frame can be found in Carolingian illumination, for example in the Bible of San

198
David and musicians.
Bible of San Paolo fuori le mura.
Reims (?), c. 870–880

Paolo fuori le mura (fig. 198). However, the motifs there (a conglomeration of roofs, turrets and walls) still appear as distant views of a city beyond the framing arch, rather than as a massive crowning baldachin. With the elimination of illusionistic space in post-Carolingian painting, the architectural *Fata Morgana* above the arcade arch loses the character of a prospect. Every detail of the composition now lies within the same surface – that is, contained on the page of the book.

To place the multi-turreted façade of the Norman miniature in its true historical perspective, it must be seen as a parallel phenomenon to the *homme-arcade*, which became popular at exactly the same time in early Romanesque sculpture (fig. 199). In relief sculpture, the human figure was incorporated into the façade by means of the arcade; in the illuminated book, by the same process, it is the constraint of the arcade that integrates the figure with the page. The imaginary architecture equates the page with structured space which, like real architecture, can harbour single figures and scenes. If there is now a gravitational pull downward to the foot of the page, the framed surface must still not be confused with pictorial space. The figures must be seen as the inhabitants of the architecture in the sense that they might be the inhabitants of initials in the script.

At the height of Byzantine influence and at the time of the great Bibles, for example the Winchester Bible (fig. 147), architectural framing remained very much in the shadow, only to gain new ground when the Gothic style was adopted in book-illumination; and that, as we know, was a hundred years later than the appearance of the Gothic style in architecture. The hypertrophic treatment of frames which characterizes the first large pictorial cycle of Parisian Gothic has already been mentioned in connection with the full-page pictures of the St. Louis Psalter (pl. XXVI). Every miniature is enclosed by a border wherein lurks an architectural frame. This has no representational value, no local reference. If the narrative calls for a building, then the framing roof is erected over the existing roof, apparently with no sense of *contradictio in adiecto*. Pictorial content and decorative device were here two entirely different modes.

The architectural superstructure in these instances is merely a stylized pattern, thin like a blind arcade or shallow tracery. But also this technique of page design is borrowed from real architecture: the diaphanous wall relief. The figures in Gothic miniatures do not lie heavily upon the surface of the page; they float upon it. (See, for example, the Crucifixion from the Senlis Missal [fig. 200], at the beginning of the fourteenth century). Accordingly, they are figures of extraordinary delicacy, slenderness, poise and elegance; they are ethereal. The same art which produced figures of unique monumentality in its sculpture, developed in book-illumination a diminutive format, a miniature style for the figural. That is true, however, principally of French Gothic. Neither English nor German Gothic seized upon this subtle distinction, and in the illumination of both countries, figures always remain the same as though destined for pictures in large format.

199
Angel. Relief from the ambulatory of Saint-Sernin, Toulouse. Southern France, c. 1100

200
Crucifixion.
Senlis Missal.
Paris, early 14th century

201
Christ in Majesty.
Missal and Breviary
from Châlons-sur-Marne.
Île-de-France, early 14th century

A specific peculiarity of French Gothic illumination is its use of decorative forms borrowed from architecture to ornament the pictorial field; quatrefoils and medallion-shaped tracery embellish the inner frame (fig. 200). An entire *Christ in Majesty* can be inserted into densely latticed tracery (fig. 201). Gold is no longer the preferred background; figures now appear frequently on red or blue patterned ground, as in contemporary stained glass where, incidentally, the diaphanous forms had found an especially receptive and congenial medium. Naturally, there was also a general tendency to produce books in small format, not only the pocket-editions of the University Bibles; and these were written in minute letters on parchment as thin as modern India paper. In this respect, the weightlessness of the illuminated book and that of the finely-painted surface complement one another.

The freedom which an architectural superstructure creates for narrative and pictorial elements can be most convincingly seen in one of the major works of Parisian illumination of the early fourteenth

century, the picture book of the Life of St. Denis in the Bibliothèque Nationale in Paris. In the miniature showing the saint preaching (fig. 202), there is a complete panorama of Paris in the buttressed architectural compartments. At the bottom of the miniature flows the river Seine; from it rises the turreted city. The higher up one goes, the larger the figures become. The scale derives from the determining perspective: distances are defined from the standpoint of the saint. Another factor may also have been at work, in that the painter, having placed heavier figures at the top of the composition, may have sought to find an equivalent balance in emphasis across the pictorial field to counterbalance the picture top and bottom. In so doing, he has also made use of the six stems of ivy sprouting from the corners and sides, to anchor the picture to the page.

The Life of St. Denis is dated 1317. Meanwhile, however, in another European centre, something revolutionary had occurred which was to affect even northern illumination deeply. It arose in Italy and consisted of a new concept of pictorial space. In the work of Giotto, a new demand was created for understanding individual details and their mutual relationships as part of a three-dimensional continuum, to interpret the topography of a still very limited pictorial space as the chief predeterminant of composition and to treat the pictorial plane – which previously had dictated all the terms of the composition – as something secondary to the phenomenon of three-dimensionality. This abrupt change had come from monumental art. The new approach applied to illumination necessarily had devastating repercussions for a layout based on the unqualified and absolute two-

202
St. Denis preaching in Paris.
Life of St. Denis.
Paris, 1317

203
Annunciation.
Hours of Jeanne of Navarre.
French, Workshop of Jean Pucelle,
second quarter of 14th century

204
Flagellation and Christ before Pilate.
Missal. School of Jean Pucelle,
mid 14th century

dimensionality of the page of the book. As a result, the very existence
of book-painting was put into jeopardy. The decisive blows in the
conflict were struck in France, where the system of design specific to
the page of the book had found its purest expression. Italy, for
example, where illumination had never or only rarely been pursued
as an end in itself, at no time created an individual style of painting
specific to the book.

One of the most revealing symptoms of the conflict is a *tendency
to reify the architectural frame*: the ornamental enclosure of the picture
is reinterpreted as a three-dimensional object, blurring the distinction
between what may simply be the frame and what may indicate where
the event takes place. I will illustrate this with four examples, all taken
from the circle of Jean Pucelle, the Parisian artist who brought the
new gospel of Giotto to France in the second quarter of the fourteenth
century. In the first example (pl. XXVIII), the pictorial field is topped
with pinnacles, buttressed against the side and resting on a platform;
in addition all this is supported by drollery figures as if by caryatids.
The picture has been given weight; it is represented as something
burdensome. In the second example (fig. 203), the decorative frame
is visualized as a house in which the Annunciation takes place. Frame
and indication of place are identical. In the third example (fig. 204),
the frame is made into a scaffold to provide a two-storied theatrical
set for the staging of several episodes from the Passion (the Flagellation
and Christ before Pilate). In the fourth example (pl. XXIX), the shallow
frame, with its inner compartmental divisions, is decorated like a
frontal of goldsmiths' work, a shrine, embellished with a Christ in

205
Christ in Majesty.
Très Belles Heures du duc de Berry.
Jacquemart de Hesdin,
early 15th century

Majesty. The subject of the miniature is not a straightforward vision
of Christ in Majesty, but rather an ornamented cult object incorporat-
ing a *Majestà*. The frontal orientation inherent in the subject does not
arise from any two-dimensional design of the page, but from the fact
that we see the front of a three-dimensional object. So it is uninten-
tional if the frontality of the composition appears to us as archaic.

It is particularly instructive to pursue this metaphysical theme of
Christ in Majesty: already in Carolingian times it had been subject to
rigid rules of composition, which had continued to be adhered to.
We can follow the development up to the point where metaphysical
Heaven becomes equated with physical heights, thus dispatching the
incarnation of divinity back to the clouds from which it had originally
descended. In one of the most lavishly illuminated Books of Hours
made for the Duc de Berry, that unrivalled bibliophile and patron,
there appears a Christ in Majesty (fig. 205) completely devoid of

206
Original design for
Christ in Majesty (seen in fig. 205).
Très Belles Heures du duc de Berry.
French, late 14th century

architectural frame and even without the usual compartmentalization of the field. But what we see today was not the original design. On the reverse of this folio, the traditional Gothic lozenge arrangement (fig. 206) is visible, obviously designed by the man responsible for the series of pictures executed about 1400. But the miniaturist who finally painted them belonged to a younger generation and, finding the old lozenge pattern unacceptable, he painted out the whole pictorial field in blue – the blue air in which the Almighty hovers, borne by a fiery glory of angels. For the symbols of the Evangelists, the illuminator with a kind of hardy logic put winged figures in the sky, and under the feet of the quadrupeds a clod of earth. The pictorial field is again an imaginary space which reaches from Earth to Heaven.

207
Mass for the Dead.
Hours by the Boucicaut Master,
first quarter of 15th century

This marks a turning point. As the pictorial field becomes pictorial space, and the frame of the picture a casing for figures which inhabit it, so the surface in between is changed to an opening through which a view of the interior is glimpsed, behind the page of the book, as in a peep-show whose curtain has been drawn aside. The penetration of the page creates a hollow space, an interior space. Herein lies one of the roots of the origin of interior painting proper, with its attendant illusion that only what can be seen within its four walls is visible. Remnants of earlier pictorial practice still stood in the way of this modern conception. Trecento illusion, where interior space was presented as an exterior view with an opening at the front, continued to exercise an influence in the North (fig. 207). For a long time the idea of indicating complete buildings was still practised, even when it was a matter only of an interior scene. In northern illumination, showing at least part of the exterior to frame the view into the interior was retained for yet another reason. Here was the final vestige of that decorative frame whose function it was to bind the picture and its space firmly to the plane of the page. And thus one will find at this point of development (that is at the beginning of the fifteenth century) few representations of space which do not show the arched opening on the outside, even when the subject is only an interior. It is really only another form of the old decorative frame.

An ingenious artist, one of the brothers Van Eyck, found a way of integrating even this last relic of convention with the new perspective. In the Mass for the Dead in the Turin Book of Hours (fig. 208), he makes us believe that the Mass takes place in the choir of a church whose transept is still in the process of being built. Consequently,

208
Mass for the Dead.
Turin Book of Hours.
Master of the Turin Prayer Book,
Flanders, second decade of 15th century

what we actually see is a fragment of a church, which is all that then existed; and this does not offend the logic of simultaneous interior and exterior viewing. The artist carries the game of the illusion even further by letting the structure emerge at the top above a simple pictorial frame, a narrow gold strip. The sectioned faces of the vault establish the picture as a cross-section; cutting across the frame defines it as a detail-section. Thus, on the inner side of the pictorial frame, the interior of the building can be seen; outside it, the exterior of the building. It is not entirely clear whether the illusion is also intended, that one is shown in front of, and the other behind the picture's plane, namely the page.

The necessity of having to look *into* the page of the book, however cleverly contrived, meant that from now on the book housed a picture *as an alien body* on which it no longer had any formal influence. Some miniaturists, with great difficulty, tried to reconcile the three-dimensionality of the picture with the flat surface of the page by using naturalistic, ivy-leaf borders, while other contemporaries tried to reshape the frame completely to bring it into harmony with the new spatial perspective. The art of the book had reached an acute crisis. Each of the three skills collectively necessary for producing an illuminated manuscript – that of illuminator, of scribe, and of decorator who held a position somewhere between the two ('enlumineur' in French terminology of the time distinguished him from 'historieur', the painter of the actual pictures in a book) – each had an entirely disparate relationship to the page: looking and reading had become two essentially distinct activities. The eye could no longer wander freely across what had previously been static and immobile, now the image was sometimes on 'optical' ground, and at other times on a 'real' one.

There was no shortage of efforts to find a *modus vivendi,* and even in the fifteenth century genuine book-illumination was achieved through ingenious illusionism, that is, painting which was not merely an imitation of panel painting but germane to the specific requirements of its medium. The names of Fouquet in France, and the Master of Mary of Burgundy in the Netherlands,[61] mark the zenith of this last flowering of western illumination.

With both artists, the deeper reasons for their achievement were firstly, that they found a common system of design, a common denominator for picture, ornament and script; and secondly, that they made the surface of the page once more the principal factor for orientation. The Master of Mary of Burgundy began his revival of book illumination with a re-evaluation of borders. He wanted the frame to allow a view at close-range, as though through a window, of the nave of a church, of an interior or even of a distant landscape. Picture and border, the whole page of the book, are enclosed in one perspective (pl. XXXI). In the border, the real surface of the book is re-created and, in a clever strategy of optical illusion, it is suggested that flowers, jewels, shells and other dainties are strewn across the surface of the book; these are the so-called *trompe-l'œil* frames. The plane of the page is now the barrier between two spaces:

209
Scenes from the Passion of Christ.
Master of Mary of Burgundy,
Bruges, c. 1490

the imaginary space of the picture behind the page, and the space in front of it posing as real.

And what happens to the script? It remains marooned like an island in the dividing wall of space. This particular artist, however, had yet another way of harmonizing the relationship between picture and script, a device even more characteristic of illumination at this later date. The picture with its space shifts into the border zone, and in the centre, by way of a break, the page of script appears, like a placard suspended in air, often attached to the pictorial space by ropes (fig. 209). Now even the script is part of an observed space: the border here is set back into the distance, and the script in the centre appears closer so that we can read it. If early on in the Middle Ages we talked of a page of script that contained a picture, we can now say that the picture contains a page of script. The picture has triumphed over script.

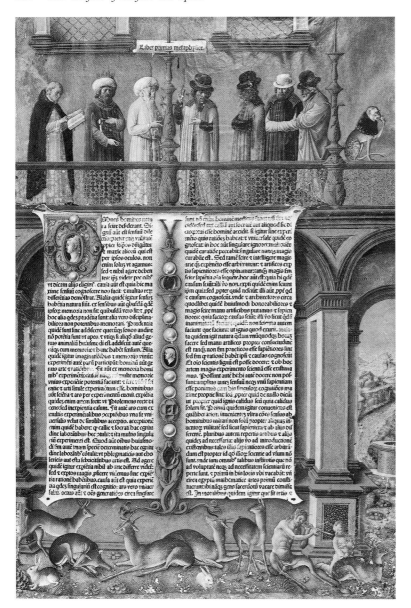

210
Title-page from Volume II
of the Works of Aristotle.
Venice, illuminated by Girolamo
da Cremona or Jacometto Veneziano;
printed by Andreas Torresanus,
Venice, 1483

Venetian illumination offers a parallel to the Netherlandish examples, and indeed one which is exactly contemporary. In an early
printed edition of Aristotle, we see the Seven Wise Men of the classical
world (eastern and western) standing on the balcony of a multi-
storied building: from its ledge hangs the first page of the *Metaphysics*
(fig. 210). A variant of this formula decorates the opening page of the
first volume of the edition (pl. XXXII). The folio appears to be torn
and ripped, allowing us a glimpse of the space behind. This intellectual
witticism can be interpreted symbolically – not only is the folio about
to fall apart, but the days of the illuminated book were themselves
numbered.

Notes

1 The reference is to M. Hauttmann, *Die Kunst des frühen Mittelalters* in *Propyläen-Kunstgeschichte,* VI (Berlin, 1929).

2 An even better example is the Crucifixion miniature in the St. Louis Psalter (Paris, Bibliothèque de l'Arsenal MS 1186, f. 24), in which not only John but Mary herself holds a book. Reproduced in H. Martin and P. Lauer, *Les principaux manuscrits à peintures de la Bibliothèque de l'Arsenal à Paris* (Paris, 1929), Pl. VIII.

3 I am referring to a 6th-century Italian manuscript from the period of St. Augustine's missionary activity.

4 The colophon was copied from an earlier codex and states that Columba took twelve days to write the book; see E. H. Zimmermann, *Vorkarolingische Miniaturen* (Berlin, 1916), p. 231.

5 The Irish King Flan commissioned a shrine *(Cumdach)* for the Book of Durrow at the beginning of the 10th century; it was lost in Trinity College Library, Dublin, around 1690.

6 Cf. *Irische Kunst aus drei Jahrtausenden, Thesaurus Hibernia,* exhibition in Cologne and Berlin (1983), catalogue no. 75. Other book shrines in catalogue nos. 76 and 83.

7 Other examples in which roll and codex both appear in the same picture are even more frequent in western illumination. One of many such examples is the Codex Millenarius, executed in Salzburg around 800, fig. 35.

8 We have a document of another type in the 'Notitia Dignitatum' – a kind of official handbook from the late Roman period – in which bundles of rolls are pictured alongside codices as the official sign of the *Magister scriniorum* (Board of Notaries). Cf. the reproduction of f. 3 in the Cambridge copy, in F. Wormald and P. Giles, *A Descriptive Catalogue of the Additional Illuminated Manuscripts in the Fitzwilliam Museum* (Cambridge, 1982), II, fig. 76. The 'Notitia Dignitatum' only survives in late medieval copies based on a Carolingian copy which was lost in the 17th century.

9 The oldest roll of this kind which still survives, and indeed is still in use, is in the possession of the Samaritans, in Nablus; reproduced in *Bibel-Lexikon,* ed. H. Haag (Einsiedeln, 1951), Pl. VII.

10 The Utrecht Psalter came to England towards the end of the first millenium. In addition to the two copies already mentioned, a third copy was made there around 1200 (Paris, Bibliothèque Nationale MS lat. 8846). In 1716 the Psalter went to Utrecht.

11 Oxford, Bodleian Library, Papyrus gr. Oxy. 2331, which contains three sketches of the Labours of Hercules, was in K. Weitzmann's opinion a significant fragment of an extensively illustrated roll; other opinions, however, regard it merely as a short satirical poem. See K. Weitzmann, *The Oxyrhynchus Papyri,* XXII (1954), p. 85 ff., Pl. XI; P. Maas, 'The ΓΡΥΛΛΟΣ Papyrus' in *Greece and Rome,* second series, V, no. 2 (October 1958), p. 171 ff.

12 Reference here is to the idea of 'Kunstwollen', coined by Alois Riegel in *Spätrömische Kunstindustrie* (Vienna, 1901). Compare further the remarks in Otto Pächt, *Methodisches zur kunsthistorischen Praxis,* ed. J. Oberhaidacher, A. Rosenauer and G. Schikola (Munich, 1986, 2nd ed.), pp. 242, 283 and 292.

13 One particular aspect is the translation of items of clothing, which were no longer the costume of the day, into contemporary fashion – a modernizing process which was a constantly recurring feature throughout medieval art.

14 K. Weitzmann, *Ancient Book Illumination* (Cambridge, Mass., 1959), and *Illustrations in Roll and Codex. A Study of the Origin and Method of Text Illumination* (Princeton, 1970, 2nd ed.).

15 F. Wickhoff, *Römische Kunst (The Vienna Genesis)* (Berlin, 1912), p. 199 ff.

16 The theological basis for the iconoclasm of the eastern Mediterranean world was established by the Synod of Hiereia in 754.

17 The typology found in the juxtapositions of the 'Biblia pauperum' and the 'Speculum humanae salvationis' constituted a specifically medieval way of thinking; it justified itself, so to speak, by quoting Christ's own words (cf. P. Durrieu, 'Les préfigures de la passion' in *Revue de l'Art chrétien,* LX, 1910, pp. 67-69), and in the course of time produced a system of thought that embraced all Holy Scripture.

18 *Vita magna s. Hugonis episcopi Lincolniensis, auct. Adam abbate,* lib. 2, cap. 13, p. 92: ... Promisit [Henricus II. rex] etiam unam bibliothecam, utriusque testamenti corpus integre continentem, se transmissurum ei. Rediit prior [Hugo] domum. Rex promissi sui non immemor, inquirit solicite bibliothecam optime confectam, quam ei conferre potuisset. Suggeritur demum studiosius quaerenti monachos s. Swithuni [Wintoniae] egregiam recenti et decenti opere confecisse bibliothecam, *in qua ad mensam edentium fratrum legi debuisset.* (O. Lehmann-Brockhaus, *Lateinische Schriftquellen zur Kunst in England, Wales und Schottland vom Jahre 901 bis zum Jahre 1307,* 2, Munich, 1956, p. 681, no. 4828).

19 Here it is the lion that symbolizes St. John and not the eagle, as established by St. Jerome.

20 In late Antiquity there were also combined title-pages for the four Gospels, inserted before the Canon Tables; for example in the Rossano Gospels, where the four Evangelists are portrayed in medallion form (reproduced in K. Weitzmann, *Late Antique and Early Christian Book Illumination,* London, 1977, Pl. XVIII). We have a counterpart to this in early western manuscripts: the Book of Kells, for example, combines the four Evangelists' symbols on ff. 27v and 129v (colour reproduction in Exh. Cat. *Irische Kunst,* [*op. cit.* n.6], pp. 10-11). Later such combined title-pages in Gospel Books are very rare.

21 From the 11th century onwards, script and picture in the Exultet Rolls were no longer in the same direction; instead they were inverted, that is to say the script is upside down if one looks at the picture, and vice and versa. The congregation assembled before the pulpit could thus see the illustration the right way up when the deacon let the roll unfold over the lectern during the Lesson.

22 This combination is also found in a fragment from a Carolingian Sacramentary (Paris, Bibliothèque nationale MS lat. 1141, f. 6 v). In the same manuscript, for the first time to my knowledge, the Preface opening also shows a move away from a purely decorative letter towards a picture (f. 5); colour reproduction in F. Mütherich, *Carolingian Painting* (London, 1977), Pls. 33 and 34.

23 *Innocentii III Papae De Sacro Altaris mysterio libri sex,* lib. III, Cap. II; *De his quorum memoria colitur in secreta* (*Patrologia Latina* 217, 840/841); the full quotation: Propter quod inter praefationem et canonem in plerisque sacramentariis imago Christi depingitur, ut non solum intellectus litterae, vero etiam aspectus picturae memoriam Dominicae passionis inspiret. Et forte divina factum est providentia licet humana non sit industria procuratum, ut ab ea littera T canon inciperet quae sui forma signum crucis ostendit et exprimit in figura. T namque mysterium crucis insinuat dicente domine per prophetam: Signa Thau in frontibus virorum dolentium et gementium (Ezech. IX).

24 *Joannes Belethus Theologus parisiensis Rationale Divinorum officiorum* Cap. XLIII, *De secunda parte missae* (*Patrologia Latina* 202, 53): Invenitur autem ibi quaedam figurae ad similitudinem nostrorum delta, D scilicet undique clausum, quod in parte praecendenti V nostrum complectitur, quod in summitate apertum est, in quorum parte medio tractulus per transversum ducitur, utramque in modum crucis partem copulans. Quod quidem non sine causa factum est. Per delta enim circulariter clausum, divina figuratur natura, quae nec principium nec finem habuit. Per V exprimitur humana Christi natura, quae principium in Virgine habuit, sed fine carebit. At vero tractulus in medio utramque partem conjungens, crux est per quam humana sociantur divinis.

25 Guilelmus Durandus, *Rationale Divinorum Officiorum,* Lib. IIII, Cap. XXXIII, De praefatione (Io. Bapt. Buysson, Lyon, 1592, p. 278): ... Ideo ergo haec figura in praefationis principio ponitur, quia per mysterium unionis & domini passionis pacificantur homines angelis, & sociatur humana divinis, in praeconia Salvatoris ...

26 Reproductions in L. A. Dournovo, *Miniatures arméniennes* (Erewan, 1967), Pls. 51, 60, 63 and 74.

27 J. Strzygowski, *Der Dom zu Aachen und seine Entstellung. Ein kunstwissenschaftlicher Protest* (Leipzig, 1904), p. 53 ff. The question of the connection between western and eastern fish/bird letters was discussed in summary by C. Nordenfalk, *Die spätantiken Zierbuchstaben* (Stockholm, 1970), p. 202 ff.

28 For example, those of the Kennicott Bible (Oxford, Bodleian MS Kennicott 1, f. 447), dated 1476, reproduced in J. Gutmann, *Hebrew Manuscript Painting* (London, 1978, fig. IX), and cf. further Pl. 10, a Bible from Cervera in Spain, 1300, now in Lisbon, Biblioteca Nacional MS 72, f. 449. In both instances it is an illuminator's colophon.

29 A variant of this initial form, the so-called gymnastic initial, in which the figures on the shaft of the letter replace the scrollwork (fig. 139), was to achieve great significance later (see p. 134 ff.).

30 Cf. also Rouen, Bibliothèque Municipale MS 456 (St. Augustine's Commentary on the Psalms), f. 1, reproduced in J. J. G. Alexander, *The Decorated Letter* (London, 1978), p. 16, Pl. 10.

31 O. Pächt, C. R. Dodwell and F. Wormald, *The St. Albans Psalter,* (London, 1960).

32 Aliud est picturam adorare, aliud per picture historiam quid sit adorandum addiscere ... (p. 68), *Gregorii I papae Registrum Epistolarum* tom. II, in *Monumenta Germaniae Historica* (Berlin, 1895), p. 269 ff. (Lib. XI, Ep. XIII: *Gregorius Sereno episcopo Massiliensi*).

33 Some volumes are too heavy to be lifted by one person; it takes three people to move the Bohemian Codex Gigas in Stockholm, c. 1200-1225, Kungliga Bibliotheket MS A. 148.309. See G. Böcker, *Illuminerade medeltida handskrifter i dansk och svensk ägo* (Stockholm, 1952), cat. no. 27.

34 Michaelbeuren, Stiftsbibliothek Cod. perg. 1, second quarter of the 12th century. See W. Cahn, *Romanesque Bible Illumination* (London, 1982), cat. no. 14, figs. 113-116.

35 One of the ways in which the Byzantine vocabulary of forms was transmitted was through the portable 'minor' arts; another was through monumental painting, such as the direct inspiration of the byzantinizing style of Norman Sicily.

36 Oxford, Bodleian Library, MS Auct. F.2.13, executed at St. Albans around the middle of the 12th century. See C. M. Kauffmann, *Romanesque Manuscripts 1066-1190* (London, 1975), pp. 17, 102, figs. 198-202.

37 The earliest appearance of gold in manuscript illumination is found in an Insular book, a Codex Aureus from Christ Church, Canterbury, dated about the middle of the 8th century, Stockholm, Kungliga Bibliotheket MS A. 135, discussed and reproduced in C. Nordenfalk, *Celtic and Anglo-Saxon Painting* (London, 1977), pp. 96-107.

38 Chrysography in the sense of gold script occurs in the Carolingian period, with similar use of gold in ornamental art; see, for example, the Drogo Sacramentary (pl. XII) or the Dagulf Psalter (pls. VIII, IX), as well as in manuscripts of the Franco-Saxon school.

39 Dante, *Divina Commedia, Purgatorio,* Canto XI, v. 80 f.

40 Canon Tables – tables of concordance for the Gospels compiled by Eusebius of Caesarea (d. 339/340) – appear with ornamental frames in the form of arcades since the 6th century. See C. Nordenfalk, *Die spätantiken Kanontafeln* (Göteborg, 1938).

41 Frames surrounding script, which include Christian symbols (the Cross, Dove, etc.), are found *inter alia* on two title-pages, f. 1 (Eusebius) and f. 7 (Rufinus Aquileiensis) in a 6th-century manuscript from Ravenna, Vienna, Österreichische Nationalbibliothek, Cod. 847. See H. J. Hermann, *Die illuminierten Handschriften und Inkunabeln der Nationalbibliothek in Wien,* I (Leipzig, 1923), pp. 39-42, Pls. VII, X.

42 Oxford, Bodleian Library, MS Canon. Class. Lat. 161, Solinus, *Polystoria,* title-page by Leonardo Bellini or his circle, Padua (?), 1457. See O. Pächt, 'Notes and Observations on the Origin of Humanistic Book-Decoration', in *Fritz Saxl 1890-1948, A Volume of Memorial Essays,* ed. D. J. Gordon (London, 1957), pp. 184-194; and O. Pächt and J. J. G. Alexander, *Illuminated Manuscripts in the Bodleian Library Oxford,* II: Italian School, (Oxford, 1970), No. 603, Pl. LVII, with further bibliography. A survey of title-pages of Humanist origin will be found in M. Corbett, 'The Architectural Title-page', *Motif* XII (1964), pp. 49-52.

43 *Die Buchillustration im 18. Jahrhundert. Colloquium der Arbeitsstelle 18. Jahrhundert, Gesamthochschule Wuppertal* (Heidelberg, 1980), illustrations on pp. 81, 82 and 241.

44 Piranesi's title-page for 'Prima parte di architetture e prospettive', first ed. 1743, reproduced in exh. cat., *Piranesi. Incisioni, rame, legature, architteture* (Venice, 1978), figs. 31 and 32.

45 *Clavis physicae* by Honorius Augustodunensis, Paris, Bibliothèque Nationale MS lat. 6734; see M. T. d'Alverny, 'Le cosmos symbolique du xiie siècle', in *Archives d'histoire doctrinale et littéraire du moyen-âge*, 28 (1954), pp. 31-83; and J. Zahlten, 'Creatio mundi. Darstellungen der sechs Schöpfungstage und naturwissenschaftliches Weltbild im Mittelalter', *Stuttgarter Beiträge zur Geschichte und Politik*, 13 (1979), fig. 278.

46 H. Liebeschütz, *Das allegorische Weltbild der heiligen Hildegard von Bingen* (Leipzig–Berlin, 1930), p. 12, n. 1.

47 *Ibid.*, p. 12.

48 *Ibid.*, p. 13.

49 Mozarabic art originated at the same time as the new, that is Romanesque monumental sculpture made its appearance, for instance in the sculpture at Silos. Thus a Romanesque style of sculpture collided here with a pre-Carolingian style of illumination.

50 The most important illustrations of the Apocalypse were executed in England in the 13th century; in the 14th century it was in France; and in the 15th century Germany was the leader, the high point being Albrecht Dürer's series of woodcuts.

51 In manuals on iconography a distinction is made between Old and New Testament subjects and secular subjects. For an analysis of pictorial narrative techniques, however, still other types are important, such as subjects from religious prose and poetry. This group naturally requires other modes of narrative and illustration than those used in accounts of history or of the lives of saints. Three literary sources, above all others, exercised the strongest influence on the Middle Ages: the Apocalypse, the Psychomachia (not discussed here) and the Psalter.

52 Pieter Bruegel, 'The Netherlandish Proverbs', Berlin, Staatliche Museen Preußischer Kulturbesitz, Inv. 1720, signed below on the right BRUEGEL 1559. See F. Grossmann, *Pieter Bruegel* (London, 1966), pl. 13.

53 No good examples have survived. The Utrecht Psalter itself testifies to this lost Byzantine tradition.

54 In the matter of word illustration, naturally the text used is of decisive importance. For the most part, however, texts were never translated literally: the German translation may frequently not match the Latin version which can in turn differ from the Greek. What has been established is that the textual basis for the Carolingian Psalter was both the translation of St. Jerome as well as a still earlier pre-Jerome version (the illustrations make no sense if one interprets them only from Jerome's translation). The textual model was probably a 'Psalterium duplex' (two parallel versions of the Psalter).

The numbering of the 150 (or 151) Psalms varies. In the Vulgate (used for reference in this book) and the Septuagint, Psalms 11 to 147 fall one number behind that of the Jewish so-called 'Massoretic Text', edited in the last quarter of the millenium; the new German standard translation equally falls one number behind.

55 This must apply to the Lindisfarne Gospels (figs. 85, 91, 92 and 181), said to be written by Eadfrith, Bishop of Lindisfarne, and also the Trier Gospels, which the illuminator signed 'Thomas scripsit', most definitely not just a reference to the scribe. Further, the Cutbercht Gospels from Salzburg were both written and painted by an Insular artist. See C. Nordenfalk, *Celtic and Anglo-Saxon Painting* (London, 1977), pls. 15-22: Lindisfarne Gospels (before 689), London, British Library Cotton MS Nero D.iv pls. 29-31; Trier Gospels (around 730), Trier, Dombibliothek 61/134. See also H. J. Hermann (*op. cit.* n. 41), p. 50 ff., Pls. xi-xx: Cutbercht Gospels (around 770), Vienna, Österreichische Nationalbibliothek Cod. 1224.

56 M. Dvořák, *Idealismus und Naturalismus in der gotischen Skulptur und Malerei* (Berlin, 1918).

57 There is a detailed discussion of the problem in W. F. Volbach, *Elfenbeinarbeiten der Spätantike und des frühen Mittelalters* (Mainz, 1976, 3rd ed.), p. 129. See further, O. Zastrow, *Museo d'arti applicate. Gli avori* (Castello Sforzesco Milano, 1978); R. Bergmann, *Salerno Ivories, Ars sacra from Medieval Amalphi* (Harvard University Press, 1980).

58 Rouen, Bibliothèque Municipale MS Y. 6., f. 29 v, 'Missal' of Robert of Jumièges, Anglo-Saxon, c. 1020.

59 H. Jantzen, *Ottonische Kunst* (Munich, 1947), p. 68 ff.

60 For a discussion on this new narrative style, see esp. O. Pächt's contribution in *The St. Albans Psalter* (*op. cit.*, n. 31).

61 O. Pächt, *The Master of Mary of Burgundy* (London, 1948).

List of Illustrations

Select Bibliography

The following selection is based on more recent publications which contain useful bibliographies.

Literature on particular Periods, Artists or Works from the Late Antique to the Renaissance

Weitzmann, K., Late Antique and Early Christian Book Illumination. London 1977

Wiener Genesis. Illuminierte Purpurhandschrift aus dem 6. Jahrhundert. Facsimile edition. Commentary by Otto Mazal. Frankfurt am Main 1980

Josua-Rolle. Complete facsimile edition of the Codex Vaticanus Palatinus Graecus 431 in the Vatican Library. Commentary by Otto Mazal. Graz 1984

Grabar A. & Nordenfalk, C., Early Medieval Painting from the fourth to the eleventh century. Lausanne 1957

Rickert, M., Painting in Britain: the Middle Ages. Harmondsworth 1954, 2nd edition 1965

Alexander, J. J. G., Insular Manuscripts 6th-9th Century. London 1978

Backhouse, J., The Lindisfarne Gospels. Oxford 1981

Henry, F., The Book of Kells. The Book and its Decoration. London 1974

Nordenfalk, C., Celtic and Anglo-Saxon Painting: Book Illumination in the British Isles, 600-800. London 1977

Dodwell, C. R., Painting in Europe 800 to 1200. Harmondsworth 1971

Porcher, J., French Miniatures from Illuminated Manuscripts. London 1959

Williams, J., Early Spanish Manuscript Illumination. London 1977

Mütherich, F. & Gaehde, J. E., Carolingian Painting. London 1977

Unterkirchner, F., Zur Ikonographie und Liturgie des Drogo-Sakramentars. Graz 1977

Temple, E., Anglo-Saxon Manuscripts 900-1066. London 1976

Wormald, F., the Benedictional of St. Ethelwold. London 1959. Reprinted in: F. Wormald, Collected Writings I. Studies in Medieval Art from the Sixth to the Twelfth Century. London-Oxford 1984, pp. 85-100

The Golden Age of Anglo-Saxon Art. Exhibition Catalogue ed. by Backhouse, J., Turner D. H. & Webster, L. London 1984

Grodecki, L., Mütherich, F., Taralon, J. & Wormald, F., Die Zeit der Ottonen und Salier (Universum der Kunst). Munich 1973 (Part 2, pp. 82-255, Die Malerei)

Kauffmann, C. M., Romanesque Manuscripts 1066-1190. London 1975

Oursel, Ch., Miniatures Cisterciennes (1109-1134). Macon 1960

Dodwell, C. R., The Canterbury School of Illumination 1066-1200. Cambridge 1954

English Romanesque Art 1066-1200. Exhibition Catalogue. London 1984

Pächt, O., Dodwell, C. R. & Wormald, F., The St. Albans Psalter (Albani Psalter). London 1960

Thomson, R. M., Manuscripts from St. Albans Abbey 1066-1235. Bury St. Edmunds 1982, 2 volumes

Morgan, N. J., Early Gothic Manuscripts (1) 1190-1250. London 1982

Marks, R. & Morgan, N., The Golden Age of English Manuscript Painting, 1200-1500. New York 1981

Avril, F., Manuscript Painting at the Court of France: the fourteenth century, 1310-1380. London 1978

Meiss, M., French Painting in the Time of Jean de Berry, I. The Late Fourteenth Century and the Patronage of the Duke. London-New York 1967, 2 volumes

Meiss, M., French Painting in the Time of Jean de Berry, II. The Boucicaut Master. London 1968

Meiss, M., French Painting in the Time of Jean de Berry, III. The Limbourgs and their Contemporaries. London 1974, 2 volumes

Thomas, M., The Golden Age: Manuscript Painting at the Time of Jean, Duc de Berry. London 1979

Pächt, O., The Master of Mary of Burgundy. London 1948

Alexander, J. J. G., Italian Renaissance Illuminations. London 1977

Amstrong, L., Renaissance Miniature Painters. The Master of the Putti and his Venetian Workshop. London 1981

Literature on particular Chapters and Themes

THE INITIAL

Alexander, J. J. G., The Decorated Letter. London 1978

Gutbrod, J., Die Initiale in Handschriften des achten bis dreizehnten Jahrhunderts. Stuttgart 1965

Nordenfalk, C., Die spätantiken Zierbuchstaben. Stockholm 1970, 2 volumes

THE BIBLE

Cahn, W., Romanesque Bible Illustration. Ithaca 1982

Oakeshott, W., The Artists of the Winchester Bible. London 1965

Oakeshott, W., The Two Winchester Bibles. Oxford 1981

THE APOCALYPSE

Harnischfeger, E., Die Bamberger Apokalypse. Stuttgart 1983

James, M. R., The Apocalypse in Art. London 1931

van der Meer, F., The Apocalypse. Visions from the Book of Revelation in Western Art. London 1978

Douce Apocalypse. Full facsimile of Oxford Bodleian Library Ms. Douce 180 with commentary by P. Klein. Endzeiterwartung und Ritter-Ideologie. Graz 1981 and 1985

THE PSALTER

Der Nersessian, S., L'illustration des psautiers grecs du moyen âge, II, Londres, Add. 19352. Paris 1970

DeWald, E. T., The Illustrations of the Utrecht Psalter. Princeton-London-Leipzig 1932

Haseloff, G., Die Psalterillustration im 13. Jahrhundert. Studien zur Geschichte der Buchmalerei in England, Frankreich und den Niederlanden. Kiel 1938

Wormald, F., The Utrecht Psalter. Utrecht 1953. Reprinted in: F. Wormald, Collected Writings I. Studies in Medieval Art from the Sixth to the Twelfth Century. London-Oxford 1984, pp. 36-46

Otto Pächt Bibliography

Writings on book illumination,
in chronological sequence

A Bohemian Martyrology. In: The Burlington Magazine, 73, London 1938, pp. 192-204.

Jean Fouquet: A study of his style. In: Journal of the Warburg and Courtauld Institutes, 4, London 1940/41, pp. 85-102.

A Book of Hours by Jean Fouquet. In: The Bodleian Library Record, I, Oxford 1941, pp. 245-247.

A Giottesque Episode in English Medieval Art. In: Journal of the Warburg and Courtauld Institutes, 6, London 1943, pp. 51-70 (reprinted in: England and the Mediterranean Tradition, Oxford 1945, pp. 40-59).

Holbein and Kratzer as Collaborators. In: The Burlington Magazine, 84, London 1944, pp. 134-139).

The Master of Mary of Burgundy. In: The Burlington Magazine, 85, London 1944, pp. 295-300.

Two Manuscripts of Ellinger, Abbot of Tegernsee. In: The Bodleian Library Record, 2, Oxford 1947, pp. 184-185.

The Master of Mary of Burgundy, London 1948.

Italian Illuminated Manuscripts from 1400-1550. Catalogue of an exhibition in the Bodleian Library, Oxford 1948 (Catalogue entries by O. Pächt), Oxford 1948.

Anglo-Saxon Studies on Illumination. Supplement to the Bibliography 1939/1945. In: Scriptorium, 3, Antwerp–Brussels 1949, pp. 159-160.

Hugo Pictor. In: The Bodleian Library Record, 3, Oxford 1950, pp. 96-103.

Early Italian Nature Studies and the Early Calendar Landscape. In: Journal of the Warburg and Courtauld Institutes, 13, London 1950, pp. 13-47 (reprinted in: The Garland Library of Art, Vol. 5, Medieval Art. New York, 1979).

Giovanni da Fano's Illustrations for Basinio's Epos Hesperis. In: Studi Romagnoli, 2, Faenza 1951, pp. 91-111.

Byzantine Illumination, Oxford 1952 (Bodleian Picture Books, No. 8).

Eine wiedergefundene Tacuinum-Sanitatis-Handschrift. In: Münchner Jahrbuch der bildenden Kunst, 3rd Series, 3/4, Munich 1952/53, pp. 172-180.

Flemish Art 1300-1700. Winter Exhibition, 1953/54. Royal Academy of Arts (Catalogue of the illuminated manuscripts by O. Pächt), London 1953.

An unknown Cycle of Illustrations of the Life of Joseph. In collaboration with Jeanne Pächt. In: Cahiers Archéologiques, 7, Paris 1954, pp. 35-49.

Die Anfänge der humanistischen Buchdekoration. Paper given at the Conference 'Ursprünge und Anfänge der Renaissance', Munich, March 1954. In: Kunstchronik, 7, Munich 1954, p. 147.

C.R. Dodwell, The Canterbury School of Illumination, Cambridge 1954. Review. In: The Oxford Magazine, Oxford 1955, p. 298.

A Forgotten Manuscript from the Library of the Duc de Berry. In: The Burlington Magazine, 98, London 1956, pp. 146-153.

René d'Anjou et les Van Eyck. In: Cahiers de l'Association internationale des études françaises, Paris 1956, pp. 41-57.

The Illustrations of St. Anselm's Prayers and Meditations. In: Journal of the Warburg and Courtauld Institutes, 19, London 1956, pp. 68-83.

Un tableau de Jacquemart de Hesdin? In: Revue des Arts, 6, Paris 1956, pp. 149-160.

Notes and Observations on the Origin of Humanistic Book-Decoration. In: Fritz Saxl, 1890-1948. A Volume of Memorial Essays from his friends in England, London 1957, pp. 184-194.

Ephraimillustration, Haggadah und Wiener Genesis. In: Festschrift für Karl M. Swoboda, Vienna, 1959, pp. 213-221.

The St. Albans Psalter. In collaboration with C.R. Dodwell and F. Wormald. The full-page miniatures by O. Pächt, London 1960 (Studies of the Warburg Institute, 25).

H. Buchthal, Miniature Painting in the Latin Kingdom of Jerusalem, Oxford 1957. Review. In: Medium Aevum, 29, Oxford 1960, pp. 151-154.

A Cycle of English Frescoes in Spain. In: The Burlington Magazine, 103, London 1961, pp. 166-175.

The Rise of Pictorial Narrative in Twelfth-Century England, Oxford 1962.

Zur Entstehung des 'Hieronymus im Gehäus'. In: Pantheon, 21, Munich, 1963, pp. 131-142.

The Limbourgs and Pisanello. In: Essais en l'honneur de Jean Porcher. Gazette des Beaux Arts, 6. Pér., 62, Paris 1963, pp. 109-122.

I. Ragusa, R. B. Green, Meditations on the Life of Christ, Princeton 1961. Review. In: Medium Aevum, 32, Oxford 1963, pp. 234-236.

The Pre-Carolingian Roots of Early Romanesque Art. In: Romanesque and Gothic Art. Studies in Western Art. Acts of the 20th International Congress of History of Art, New York 1961, Vol. 1, Princeton 1963, pp. 67-75.

Vita Sancti Simperti. Eine Handschrift für Maximilian I. Berlin 1964.

Illuminated Manuscripts in the Bodleian Library Oxford, I. German, Dutch, Flemish, French and Spanish Schools. In collaboration with J.J.G. Alexander, Oxford 1966.

Illuminated Manuscripts in the Bodleian Library Oxford, II. Italian School. In collaboration with J.J.G. Alexander, Oxford 1970.

Der Weg von der zeichnerischen Buchillustration zur eigenständigen Zeichnung. In: Wiener Jahrbuch für Kunstgeschichte, 24, Vienna, 1971, pp. 178-184.

Illuminated Manuscripts in the Bodleian Library Oxford, III. British, Irish and Icelandic Schools. In collaboration with J.J.G. Alexander, Oxford 1973.

Die illuminierten Handschriften und Inkunabeln der Österreichischen Nationalbibliothek, 1. Französische Schule I, two vols., Vienna 1974. In collaboration with Dagmar Thoss. (Österr. Akad. d. Wissenschaften. Veröffentl. d. Komm. f. Schrift- u. Buchwesen d. Mittelalters, Series 1, Vol. 1.)

Historiae Romanorum. Cod. 151 in scrin. der Staatsbibliothek Hamburg, Berlin 1974. In collaboration with Tilo Brandis.

René d'Anjou-Studien. Part 1. In: Jahrbuch der kunsthistorischen Sammlungen in Wien, 69, 1973 (Vienna 1974), pp. 85-126.

Die illuminierten Handschriften und Inkunabeln der Österreichischen Nationalbibliothek, 3. Holländische Schule. Two vols., Vienna 1975. In collaboration with Ulrike Jenni. (Österr. Akad. d. Wissenschaften. Veröffentl. d. Komm. f. Schrift- u. Buchwesen d. Mittelalters, Series 1, Vol. 3.)

Die früheste abendländische Kopie der Illustrationen des Wiener Dioskurides. Für Hugo Buchthal zum 65. Geburtstag. In: Zeitschr. f. Kunstgeschichte, 38, Munich, Berlin 1975, pp. 201-214.

Francis Wormald, The Winchester Psalter, London 1973. Review. In: Kunstchronik, 28, Munich 1975, pp. 175-182.

Die niederländischen Stundenbücher des Lord Hastings. In: Litterae textuales. Essays presented to G. I. Lieftinck, 4, Amsterdam 1976, pp. 28-32.

Die illuminierten Handschriften und Inkunabeln der Österreichischen Nationalbibliothek, 2. Französische Schule II. Two vols., Vienna 1977. In collaboration with Dagmar Thoss. (Österr. Akad. d. Wissenschaften, Veröffentl. d. Komm. f. Schrift- u. Buchwesen d. Mittelalters, Series 1, Vol. 2.)

René d'Anjou-Studien. Part 2. In: Jahrbuch der kunsthistorischen Sammlungen in Wien, 73, 1977, pp. 7-106.

'La terre de Flandres'. In: Pantheon, 36/1, Munich 1978, pp. 3-16.

'Simon Mormion myt der handt'. In: Revue de l'art, 46, 1979, pp. 7-15.

Die illuminierten Handschriften und Inkunabeln der Österreichischen Nationalbibliothek, 6, Flämische Schule 1. Two vols., Vienna 1983. In collaboration with Ulrike Jenni and Dagmar Thoss. (Österr. Akad. d. Wissenschaften, Veröffentl. d. Komm. f. Schrift- u. Buchwesen d. Mittelalters, Series 1, Vol. 6.)

Die Evangelistenbilder in Simon Benings Stockholmer Stundenbuch. In: Nationalmuseum Bulletin, 7/2, Stockholm 1983, pp. 71-92.

Glossary

Acanthus Plant from the Mediterranean region with fleshy, curling, large-lobed leaves which, more or less stylized, are used as ornament

Anthromorphic In human form

Beast columns Columns found especially in the Romanesque period, on whose shafts fighting animals, or fighting humans and animals, are represented

Benedictional Liturgical book used by Bishops. Contains episcopal benedictions for the great Feasts of the Church year, with instructions for the rites to be performed

Calligraphy; Calligrapher The art of fine handwriting; a fine scribe

Canon picture ('Kanonbild') Image of the Crucifixion preceding the Canon of the Mass, the principal prayer of the Mass

Canon table A concordance table usually arranged in columns under arches, showing parallel passages from two or more of the four Gospels

Choir books General description for the books used in Church Services containing the chants of the Latin liturgy, and arranged according to their various functions (e. g. Antiphonal, Pontifical)

Clipeus Originally a round Roman shield, later a portrait on a round shield or rimless plaque

Codex, Codices Form of book in which the leaves are not glued one to the other and then rolled together, as in the Roll, but folded, sewn and bound. In contrast to the Roll, parchment was used for this book form, the word 'Codex' having originally meant 'scraped off', referring to the prepared animal membrane. It eventually became the general term for all books handwritten on sheets of parchment

Colophon Passage appearing at the end of a manuscript, recording information about the text, place and date of execution, and occasionally name of scribe

Computistical Mathematical and astronomical means of reckoning the Calendar

Drollery Animal and human hybrids that enliven the foliate borders of Gothic

manuscript pages, and frequently also enact whole scenes

Epigraph Inscription

Evangeliary Gospel Book (q. v.)

Evangelist Symbols According to the Vision of Ezekiel (1, 5-14) and the Revelation of St. John (4, 6-8) the four Evangelists were symbolized by four winged creatures: Man (Matthew), Lion (Mark), Ox (Luke), and Eagle (John)

Evangelistary Gospel Lectionary (q. v.)

Explicit Closing words of text (in Latin, 'it ends') in a classical or medieval manuscript, either at the end of a section or at the very end of a book

Exultet Roll Roll of Script, found only in southern and central Italy, and generally illustrated, containing the liturgical text for the sanctification of the Paschal Candle on Holy Saturday, which begins with the word 'Ex(s)ultet'

Figure initial Human, animal or hybrid creatures in the shape of an initial letter

Folio volume A large-format book

Frontispiece Title-page

Gospel Book, Gospels Liturgical book containing the complete text of the Gospels of St. Matthew, St. Mark, St. Luke and St. John

Gospel Lectionary Liturgical book containing a selection of passages from the four Gospels, arranged in the order of the liturgical year, to be read during Mass

Historiated initial Initial enclosing groups of figures or narrative scenes illustrating, or referring to, the text it introduces

Iconography Pictorial tradition of a representational theme

Illuminator Decorator or painter of books

Incipit Opening words of text (in Latin, 'it begins') in late-antique or medieval manuscripts, either at the beginning of the book or the beginning of a section

Inhabited initial Initial made up of foliate scroll-work within which are small human, animal or grotesque figures

Initial Emphasized letter at the beginning of a text

Jesse Tree Genealogical diagram showing the ancestors of Christ ascending from the root of Jesse, the father of David, in the form of a tree that entwines full figures or portrait-busts among its branches

Lectionary Liturgical book containing the texts to be read during Church Services

Ligature Linked letters

Liturgy, liturgical Relating to the Divine Service

Majestas Domini Christ in Majesty – the 'Power and Glory of the Lord' from the Vision of Ezekiel and the apocalyptic image of the Risen Christ

Majuscule Capital letters, upper-case

Mandorla An almond-shaped frame, or aureole, encircling the whole body of a person – usually reserved for Christ or the Virgin

Minuscule Small script (with ascenders and descenders), lower-case

Missal Liturgical book containing the Masses for the Feast days and the Saints' days of the year

Octateuch The first eight books of the Old Testament

Pantocrator Christ, the ruler of all

Pentateuch The first five books of the Old Testament

r = recto Right side of a leaf – in manuscripts it is usual to count leaves or folios, and not pages

Sacramentary Liturgical book containing all the prayers of the Mass recited by the priest (or bishop); it was the forerunner of the Missal

Septuagint Oldest and most important translation of the Old Testament into Greek. The name goes back to the legend that it took 72 days for 72 Jews to complete the translation

Thorah The first five books of the Old Testament containing the Mosaic Law

Trumeau Central support of a large doorway

v = verso Reverse side of a leaf or folio in a manuscript

Zoomorphic In animal form

Index of Manuscripts

*Illustrations of works of art
other than manuscripts
are listed in the General Index*

General Index

Sources of Photographs

ANTELLA (Florence) Scala Istituto Fotografico: col. pl. XXIV

BARCELONA, Foto Mas: 164

BRUSSELS, Bibliothèque Royale: 183, 205, 206

CAMBRIDGE, Fitzwilliam Museum: 32

COLOGNE, Photo Wolfgang F. Meier: col. pl. XIV

FRANKFURT AM MAIN, Liebieghaus: 33

GRAZ, Akademische Druck- und Verlagsanstalt: 35, 103, 105, 106, 107, col. pls. VIII, IX, XII, XXV, XXVI, 10, 17

LONDON, British Library: 9, 152, col. pls. XVIII, XX; Courtauld Institute: 69, 116, 138, 139, 149, 174; Victoria and Albert Museum: 123; Warburg Institute: 34, 142, 146, 147, 148

MADRID, Biblioteca Nacional: 209

MANCHESTER, University of Manchester, History of Art Department: col. pl. XXIII

MARBURG, Foto Marburg: 173, 199

MUNICH, Bayerische Staatsbibliothek: col. pls. XIII, XV; Bayerisches Nationalmuseum: 104; Photo Hirmer: 108, 171; Staatliche Graphische Sammlung: 80, 81

NEW YORK, Metropolitan Museum: 101; Pierpont Morgan Library: 194, col. pl. XXI

OXFORD, Bodleian Library: 67, 112, 151, 197, col. pls. XVI, XVII, XXXI

PARIS, Bibliothèque Nationale: 23, 93, 96, 153, 157, 167, col. pl. X; Photo Giraudon: 77, 131

ROME, Biblioteca Apostolica Vaticana: 38

ROUEN, Photo Ellebé: col. pl. XIX

SALONIKA, Photo Lykides: 3, 16

ST. GALL, Photo Morscher: 98, 182

VIENNA, Kunsthistorisches Institut der Universität: 1, 15, 22, 39, 44, 45, 47, 48, 50, 52, 56, 60, 61, 62, 65, 66, 71, 72, 79, 97, 99, 102, 126, 134, 135, 140, 144, 155, 165, 170, 186, 187, 188, 196, 198, 208; Österreichische Nationalbibliothek: 8, 51, 150, 158; Photo Meyer: col. pls. VI, VII

All other photos are from the archives of the author and the publishers.

Preface to the original German Edition

This book is based on a series of lectures, 'Introduction to Medieval Illumination', delivered by Otto Pächt at the University of Vienna in the Winter term of 1967/68. To describe the contents of these lectures, one must begin by saying what they were not, and were not intended to be: that is, a history of manuscript illumination in the usual sense of an historical survey of facts and periods. Nevertheless, in another deeper sense, the result is a history of illumination, affording the reader fundamental insights into the origins, development and inherent principles of this characteristically medieval form of art, which no historical survey – however detailed and exhaustive – can convey. The author's aim has been, in the first instance, to re-awaken a true understanding of the particular nature of the art of illumination, which arises from the perpetual interplay of script, picture and ornament, and also to demonstrate visually the 'workings' of the creative artistic imagination of the medieval illuminator with a rich array of examples. Every theme discussed provides Professor Pächt with an opportunity for going beyond the purely factual, and allows him the occasion for formulating fundamental statements, for touching on major problems or tracing general lines of development. Knowledge and understanding, gained during decades of teaching and research, are here presented in a concise and comprehensive form. It is this quality which may explain why it was possible and, indeed, easy to publish a series of lectures, delivered alomost twenty years ago, in effect unchanged. The insights contained there remain valid, irrespective of any new detail discoveries.

For this publication, the author made his original manuscript available, and it was his wish that the text be left more or less in the form in which it was written – as lectures. However, some *ex tempore* interpolations, based on audience response, have been incorporated into the manuscript.* The Editors are responsible for the Notes to the Text, and in the Select Bibliography they have included also Professor Pächt's later and most recent writings – published since the delivery of the lectures – where these are special studies relevant to the text. The Glossary deals with specialist terms not directly explained in the book, and an Index of Manuscripts and other works is also included.

Dagmar Thoss and Ulrike Jenni

---

* *Ex tempore* remarks are indicated with brackets in the German text, but these have been eliminated in the English translation.